Ainash Khaliullinovna Davletova
Akmaral Khamzievna Kasymova
Bakhyt Zhaparovich Sharipov

Distance training of teachers to use multimedia tools and technologies

Ainash Khaliullinovna Davletova
Akmaral Khamzievna Kasymova
Bakhyt Zhaparovich Sharipov

Distance training of teachers to use multimedia tools and technologies

ScienciaScripts

Imprint
Any brand names and product names mentioned in this book are subject to trademark, brand or patent protection and are trademarks or registered trademarks of their respective holders. The use of brand names, product names, common names, trade names, product descriptions etc. even without a particular marking in this work is in no way to be construed to mean that such names may be regarded as unrestricted in respect of trademark and brand protection legislation and could thus be used by anyone.

Cover image: www.ingimage.com

This book is a translation from the original published under ISBN 978-620-2-07284-7.

Publisher:
Sciencia Scripts
is a trademark of
Dodo Books Indian Ocean Ltd. and OmniScriptum S.R.L publishing group

120 High Road, East Finchley, London, N2 9ED, United Kingdom
Str. Armeneasca 28/1, office 1, Chisinau MD-2012, Republic of Moldova, Europe
Printed at: see last page
ISBN: 978-620-7-79468-3

Table of Contents

Introduction

The present methodical manual is oriented on preparation of teachers for reasonable and effective use of multimedia tools and technologies in distance learning of teachers, graduate students and undergraduates.

It considers the specifics of multimedia application in the main types of educational activities. The use of the methodical manual will allow to familiarize teachers with the main technical and software tools of multimedia, as well as their classification, technologies for creating educational hypermedia resources, the system of multimedia resources and methods used in distance learning for teachers, as well as approaches to determining the quality of multimedia resources. The content of the publication includes requirements for teachers developing and using multimedia resources.

Effective use of modern means of information and communication technologies in general secondary education is impossible without appropriate training and retraining of teachers, undergraduates and students.

No matter how well equipped schools are with computer equipment, access to global telecommunication systems, modern electronic publications and resources, the practical effect of using all these innovations will be minimal without the appropriate knowledge, skills and motivation of teachers.

One of the directions of teachers' professional development should be their familiarization with the most widespread and effective information resources and technologies from the point of view of their use in education. Multimedia is one of the most important among such resources and technologies.

The development of the information services industry of the education sector, including the production and publication of educational and methodological multimedia materials for teachers, along with the creation and development of telecommunication structures of individual educational institutions and the industry as a whole forms the basis for the formation of the infrastructure of informatization of education.

Teachers should master the multifariousness of the concept of multimedia and the specificity of pedagogical application of multimedia in all its meanings, namely as a technology describing the order of development, functioning and application of information processing tools of different types, products created on the basis of multimedia technology, multimedia computer program, computer hardware, a special generalizing type of information that combines information of different types.

The content of the methodical manual includes sections devoted to the peculiarities of organizing a dialogue between a person and a multimedia resource, areas and pedagogical scenarios of multimedia application in general secondary education, aspects of increasing students' motivation for learning when using multimedia at school.

The content of the manual is based on the works of famous Russian scientists - *Grigoriev Sergey Georgievich* - Doctor of Technical Sciences, Professor *and*

Grinshkun Vadim Valerievich - Doctor of Pedagogical Sciences, Professor, who have made a great contribution to the development of the basics of multimedia resources and technology [1,2].

Chapter 1.

Theoretical and practical characteristics of multimedia resources

§ 1.1 The concept of multimedia. Multiple meanings of the concept of "multimedia". Peculiarities of multimedia use

In hardware, there is a special family of means characterized by the ability to process and present information of various types, which are relatively new in terms of the development of computer technology. Indeed, in recent years, devices for recording and reproduction of sound, photo and video images have been referred to as multimedia tools. If in the near future devices for digital processing of odors appear and become widespread, these devices will also be referred to the multimedia family.

The availability of multimedia (multi - many, media - medium) is a rich arsenal of ways to illustrate the phenomenon under study. Multimedia products use a variety of information: computer data, TV and video information, speech and music. This combination leads to the use of a variety of technical devices for recording and reproducing information, allowing control from a computer to a television set,

VCR, HiFi-audio system, CD player (OD), tape recorder and electronic musical instruments. Multimedia tools are inherently interactive, meaning that the viewer and listener of multimedia products does not remain passive. Multimedia enhances learning and keeps the attention of the learner. If previously a worn-out black-and-white film "Actions of the population in conditions of chemical alarm" shown at civil defense classes was the limit of dreams, modern technical means allow to create much more spectacular training aids in the form of computer animation or even a game.

It is impossible to understand the specifics of multimedia tools without knowing the types of information and ways of its presentation, which is the subject of computer science. Let us dwell only on the main aspects of information classification, which are important for studying the peculiarities of multimedia use in general secondary education.

There are several criteria according to which information can be classified. As a first criterion, the widespread principle of distinguishing types of human perception of information, such as sight, hearing, smell, touch, taste, can be used. From the point of view of studying informatization of education, it is reasonable to consider only those types of information impact on a person, which are possible when working with computer and communication equipment. Thus, all information by types of perception can be divided into three main groups:

1. Information perceived by human vision, so-called *visual or visual information,* including text, graphic images and drawings, photographs, cartoons, videos;

2. Information perceived by the human hearing aid, so-called *sound information,* including arbitrary noises, musical pieces, and speech;

3. Information perceived by the human sensory system, so-called *sensory or tactile information,* when working with the help of special technical means.

All of the above types of information can be classified by other criteria as well. One of them is the way a person perceives information. In this regard, all information received by the learner can be divided into associative and direct information.

Let us define *associative information* as information, the perception of which is based on associations arising in a person under the influence of previously learned information. With this approach to classification, this type of information can include text, speech, and possibly drawings and cartoons. As an example, we can give a text or verbal description of a plant, with which schoolchildren are familiarized during the study of botany. In this case, reading the text or listening to the teacher's speech leads to the association of the information with students' existing ideas about plants. It is important to realize that reading a text or listening to a speech will not lead to the same perception of a plant by all students. Each student will visualize the plant being studied in a different way.

Direct information directly conveys the properties of objects that are important, also in terms of learning objectives. This type of information may include photographs, video films, arbitrary sound, called noise in science. One of the essential distinguishing features of multimedia tools is considered to be the ability to present and process direct information. For example, the use of multimedia tools in the study of plants in the course of botany allows students to see the studied plant and the processes occurring with it, to hear possible sounds, which allows to form more correct images that best correspond to the real objects and processes with which a person deals in life.

Thus, the concept of multimedia, in general, and multimedia tools, in particular, on the one hand, is closely related to computer processing and presentation of different types of information and, on the other hand, is the basis for the functioning of multimedia tools that significantly affect the effectiveness of general secondary education. The availability and introduction of multimedia tools into mass school contributes to the emergence of appropriate computer software and their content, the development of new teaching methods and technologies of informatization of teachers' professional activity.

For example, the emergence and penetration into the system of general secondary education of multimedia tools that allow storing, processing and playing back video films has led to the creation of computer programs used in teaching that contain fragments of video films shown to schoolchildren. This, in turn, has given rise to new methodological scenarios of lessons in which pupils working with computers devote part of their teaching time to watching video fragments that are important from the point of view of learning objectives. Obviously, the video materials used in education have changed qualitatively, including through the use of appropriate multimedia tools. It is important to realize that, like many other words in the language, the word "multimedia" has several different meanings.

Multimedia is:

• a technology describing the procedure of development, functioning and application of information processing tools of different types;

• information resource created on the basis of technologies for processing and presenting information of different types;

· computer software, the functioning of which is associated with the processing and presentation of information of various types;

· computer hardware that makes it possible to work with different types of information;

· a special generalizing type of information that combines both traditional static visual (text, graphics) and dynamic information of different types (speech, music, video fragments, animation, etc.).

All of these interpretations will be used and discussed in the content of this tutorial.

Thus, in a broad sense, the term **"multimedia"** means a range of information technologies that use various software and technical means to most effectively influence the user (who becomes both reader, listener and viewer).

Due to the use of multimedia in the means of informatization due to the simultaneous impact of graphic, audio, photo and video information, such means have a great emotional charge and are actively included in the entertainment industry, the practice of various institutions, home leisure.

The emergence of multimedia systems has revolutionized many areas of human activity. One of the widest areas of application of multimedia technology is in the field of education, because the means of informatization based on multimedia can, in some cases, significantly increase the effectiveness of learning. It has been experimentally established that in case of oral presentation of material, a student perceives and is able to process up to one thousand conventional units of information per minute, and up to 100 thousand such units when the visual organs are "connected".

Multimedia tools and technologies provide an opportunity to intensify learning and increase motivation for learning through the use of modern ways of processing audiovisual information, such as:

· "manipulating" (overlaying, moving) visual information;

· contamination (mixing) of different audiovisual information;

· realization of animation effects;

· deformation of visual information (increasing or decreasing a certain linear parameter, stretching or compressing an image);

· discrete presentation of audiovisual information;

· image toning;

· fixation of a selected part of visual information for its further moving or examination "under a magnifying glass";

• multi-window presentation of audiovisual information on one screen with the ability to activate any part of the screen (for example, in one "window" a video, in another - text);

• demonstration of real processes, events in real time (video film).

There are several concepts related to multimedia and the use of relevant multimedia tools in general secondary education. In particular, the role of illustrations increases significantly when using multimedia in school education.

There are two main interpretations of the term "illustration".

Illustration (illustration) is:

• introducing explanatory or supplementary information of another type (images and sound) into the text;

• giving examples (possibly without using other types of information) to make the explanation clear and convincing.

It is important to understand that both interpretations of the term illustration are equally relevant to both conventional paper textbooks and teaching aids and modern multimedia tools of educational informatization. Moreover, the necessity of illustration leads to the fact that now all means of informatization of education should be used for visual, convincing and accessible explanation of the main, fundamental or most complex points of the educational material. Multimedia contributes to this.

In multimedia tools illustrations can be presented in the form of examples (including text), two-dimensional and three-dimensional graphic images (drawings, photos, schemes, graphs, diagrams), sound fragments, animation, video fragments.

The emergence of new types of illustrations in educational multimedia media does not mean a complete rejection of the previous approaches used in publishing traditional textbooks on paper. In the field of illustration and polygraphic design of traditional educational books, considerable experience has been accumulated, according to which the peculiarities of spatial grouping of publication elements are determined, accentuation (visual highlighting) of separate elements is carried out, physiological aspects of perception and other factors are taken into account. This experience is successfully applied in the development of modern multimedia tools designed for general secondary education.

Multimedia is an effective educational technology due to its inherent qualities of interactivity, flexibility and integration of different types of educational information, as well as due to the ability to take into account the individual characteristics of students and to increase their motivation.

Interactivity of multimedia tools means that users, usually teachers and students, are given the opportunity to actively interact with these tools. Interactivity means that there are conditions for an educational dialog, one of the participants of which is the multimedia tool.

Providing interactivity is one of the most significant advantages of multimedia tools.

Interactivity allows for a certain amount of control over the presentation of information: learners can individually change settings, examine results, and respond to program requests for specific user preferences. Learners can set the speed of presentation, the number of repetitions, and other parameters to suit individual needs. This allows us to conclude that multimedia technologies are flexible.

Multimedia technologies allow many types of information to be integrated in a meaningful and harmonious way. It allows the computer to present information in various forms such as:

· images, including scanned photographs, drawings, maps and slides;

· voice recordings, sound effects and music;

· video, complex video effects;

· Animation and animation simulation.

Multimedia can be applied in the context of a wide variety of learning styles and perceived by a wide variety of people: some prefer to learn through reading, others through listening, others through watching videos, and so on.

§ 1.2 Use of multimedia tools in teaching as a component of informatization of education

The use of multimedia allows students to work with educational materials in different ways - a person decides how to study the materials, how to apply the interactive capabilities of informatization tools, and how to implement joint work with fellow students. Thus, students become active participants of the educational process.

Working with multimedia tools, students can influence their own learning process, adjusting it to their individual abilities and preferences. They learn exactly the material they are interested in, repeat the study as many times as they need, which contributes to a more correct perception.

Thus, the use of quality multimedia tools can make the learning process flexible in relation to social and cultural differences between learners, their individual learning styles and paces, and their interests.

The use of multimedia can have a positive impact on several aspects of the learning process at once.

Multimedia facilitates:

■ stimulating cognitive aspects of learning, such as perception and comprehension of information;

■ Increasing student motivation;

■ to develop the skills of teamwork and collective learning of learners;

■ development of students to develop a deeper approach to learning, and therefore entails the formation of a deeper understanding of the material being studied.

Multimedia tools can be used to enhance learning, both in specific subject areas and in disciplines at the intersection of several subject areas.

The effectiveness of the general secondary education system is also greatly influenced by the environment in which the learning process takes place. This includes the structure of the learning process, its conditions and accessibility (society, libraries, multimedia resource centers, computer laboratories, etc.).

In such circumstances, multimedia can be used as one of many possible learning environments. This environment is applicable in numerous educational projects in which students reflect on the subject area being studied and engage in a dialog with their peers and Teachers, discussing the progress and results of their learning.

So, the development of modern multimedia tools allows to realize educational technologies at a fundamentally new level, using for these purposes the most progressive technical innovations that allow to provide and process information of various types. One of the most modern multimedia tools penetrating into the sphere of general secondary education are various modeling tools and tools, the functioning of which is based on technologies called "virtual reality".

Virtual objects or processes include electronic models of both real and imaginary objects or processes. The adjective virtual is used to emphasize the characteristics of electronic analogues of educational and other objects presented on paper and other tangible media. In addition, this characteristic means the presence of an interface based on multimedia technologies that imitates the properties of real space when working with electronic analog models.

Virtual reality is a multimedia means that provide sound, visual, tactile, and other types of information and create the illusion of entering and presence of the user in a volumetric virtual space, moving the user relative to the objects of this space in real time.

Virtual reality systems provide direct "face-to-face" human contact with the environment. In the most advanced of them, the user can touch an object that exists only in the computer's memory by wearing a glove filled with sensors. In other cases, it is possible to "flip" the object depicted on the screen and examine it from the reverse side. The user can "step" into the virtual space, armed with an "information suit", "information glove", "information glasses" (glasses-monitors) and other devices. The use of such multimedia tools at school changes the mechanism of perception and comprehension of the received information. When working with "virtual reality" systems in general secondary education, there is a qualitative change in information perception. In this case, perception is carried out not only with the help of sight and hearing, but also with the help of touch and even smell. The prerequisites for the realization of the didactic principle of visual learning at a fundamentally new level arise.

It is promising to use this multimedia technology in school education for the development of spatial concepts, for the organization of training of schoolchildren in conditions that are as close as possible to the real reality.

Comprehension of information provided by "virtual reality" systems can be not only theoretical, but also practical, namely, visual and figurative or visual and action thinking. Practical thinking requires less effort compared to theoretical thinking, perception of figurative information is usually easier than perception of symbolic information. Therefore, multimedia tools built with the use of virtual reality technology are able to provide better understanding and assimilation of educational material in the learning process. However, it is important to understand that the higher the level of virtual reality systems, the more work should be invested in their creation, the more advanced should be the technical means of informatization available to teachers and students.

§ 1.3 Advantages and disadvantages of using multimedia in teaching and learning

Multimedia technologies are penetrating more and more into various spheres of educational activity every day. This is facilitated by both external factors related to the widespread informatization of society and the need for appropriate training of schoolchildren, and internal factors related to the spread of modern computer hardware and software in general education institutions, the adoption of state and interstate programs of informatization of education, the emergence of the necessary experience of informatization in an increasing number of school teachers. In most cases, the use of multimedia tools has a positive impact on teachers' labor intensification and on the efficiency of schoolchildren's learning.

At the same time, any experienced school teacher will confirm that against the background of quite often positive effect from the introduction of information technologies, in many cases the use of multimedia tools has no effect on improving the effectiveness of learning, and in some cases such use has a negative effect. It is obvious that the solution to the problems of appropriate and justified informatization of education should be carried out comprehensively and universally.

Educators should take into account two possible directions of introducing multimedia tools into the teaching process. The first of them is connected with the fact that such tools are included in the educational process as "supporting" tools within the framework of traditional methods of the historically established school education system. In this case, multimedia resources act as a means of intensifying the learning process, individualization of learning and partial automation of teachers' routine work related to recording, measuring and evaluating students' knowledge.

The introduction of multimedia resources within the framework of the second direction leads to changes in the content of education, revision of methods and forms of organizing the learning process at school, construction of holistic courses based on the use of the content of resources in individual academic disciplines. In this case, knowledge, skills and abilities are considered not as a goal, but as a means of developing a schoolchild's personality. The use of multimedia technologies will be justified and will lead to an increase in the effectiveness of learning if such use meets the specific needs of the general secondary education system, if it is impossible or difficult to teach in full without the use of appropriate means of informatization.

Obviously, any teacher should familiarize himself/herself with several groups of such needs, defined both in relation to the teaching process itself and in relation to other spheres of teachers' activity.

The first group includes needs related to the formation of certain knowledge systems in pupils. Such needs arise when familiarizing with the content of several disciplines at once, when conducting classes of interdisciplinary nature. In addition, they arise when studying elements of the micro and macro worlds, as well as in the case of the need to study a number of concepts, theories and laws, which in traditional school education can not find the required experimental substantiation (study of weightlessness, familiarization with the concept of infinity).

The second group of needs is determined by the need for schoolchildren to master reproductive skills. The needs of this group arise in situations related to calculations (time reduction, checking and processing of results). At the same time, the needs of the second group arise when practicing typical skills for each discipline (determining the division value of measuring instruments in physics, composing isomers based on the carbon skeleton in chemistry) and when forming general learning skills (general logical - systematization and classification, analysis and synthesis, reflexive - the ability to plan an experiment, collect and analyze information).

The third group of needs is determined by the need to form creative skills in pupils (the main sign of creativity is the novelty of the obtained product). Such needs arise when solving optimization problems, in which one of a number of possible variants is chosen from a number of possible variants - the most rational from a certain point of view, when solving problems to choose the most economical solution or the most optimal variant of the process (finding the optimal solution not only mathematically, but also graphically). The needs of this group arise when setting and solving problems to test hypotheses, when it is necessary to develop constructive and combinatorial creative skills (using digital constructors that allow assembling the whole from parts, modeling objects and processes). In addition, we can also include the needs arising from the need to model processes or a sequence of events, which allows the student to draw conclusions about the factors influencing the processes or events. Finally, the third group includes needs arising from a laboratory experiment that requires instruments that are not available at a particular educational institution or for a very long (short) period of time. Such a laboratory experiment may be conducted within the framework of pedagogical measurements and also entail the need to use appropriate information and telecommunication technologies.

The fourth group of needs is connected with the need to form certain personal qualities in schoolchildren. The needs referred to the fourth group arise for the organization of modeling, creating opportunities for moral education of students through the solution of social, environmental and other problems (analysis of possible consequences of accidents, consequences of the use of various technologies, allowing not only to teach students to avoid such dangers, but also to educate moral assessment of their occurrence in the modern world). Also, the need to use multimedia can arise to form in students a sense of responsibility towards other people, towards themselves and their own bodies.

Along with the above-mentioned needs for justified and effective use of multimedia technologies it is necessary to know the main positive and negative aspects of informatization of teaching, use of multimedia resources. It is obvious that knowledge of such aspects will help to use multimedia where it entails the greatest benefits and minimize possible negative aspects associated with the work of schoolchildren with modern means of informatization.

There are many positive aspects of using information and telecommunication technologies in education (which, of course, include multimedia). The main aspects include:

■ improvement of methods and technologies of selection and formation of educational content,

■ introduction and development of new specialized academic disciplines and areas of study related to informatics and information technologies,

■ making changes in the teaching systems of most traditional school disciplines not related to informatics,

■ Increasing the effectiveness of school education through its individualization and differentiation, and the use of additional motivational levers,

■ organization of new forms of interaction in the learning process,

■ change in the content and nature of the activities of the pupil and the teacher,

■ Improvement of management mechanisms of the general secondary education system.

In addition, the advantages of using multimedia in general secondary education include:

· the simultaneous use of multiple channels of student perception in the learning process, thereby achieving the integration of information delivered by several different senses;

· The ability to simulate complex, expensive, or dangerous real-world experiments;

· visualization of abstract information through dynamic representation of processes;

· visualization of objects and processes of micro- and macro-worlds;

· opportunity to develop students' cognitive structures and interpretations by framing the material being taught in a broad academic, social, and historical context, and connecting the instructional material to the student's interpretation.

The negative aspects include the curtailment of social contacts, the reduction of social interaction and communication, individualism, the difficulty of transition from the sign form of knowledge representation on the pages of a textbook or on the display screen to the system of practical actions that have a logic different from the logic of the organization of the system of signs. In case of widespread use of multimedia technologies, teachers and students become unable to take advantage of the large amount of information provided by modern multimedia and telecommunication means. Complex ways of presenting information distract students from the material being studied.

It should be remembered that if students are shown different types of information at the same time, they are distracted from some types of information in order to keep track of others, missing important information, and the use of informatization tools often deprives students of the opportunity to conduct real experiments with their own hands.

Individualization limits the live communication between teachers and trainees, students among themselves, offering them communication in the form of "dialogue with the computer". The learner does not receive sufficient practice in dialogical communication, formation and formulation of thoughts in a professional language.

Finally, excessive and unjustified use of computer technology negatively affects the health of all participants in the educational process.

The listed problems and contradictions show that the use of multimedia resources in school teaching according to the principle "the more the better" cannot lead to a real increase in the effectiveness of the general secondary education system. The use of multimedia resources requires a balanced and well-reasoned approach.

Chapter 2.

Technical and software tools of multimedia
§ 2.1 Technical tools of multimedia. Telecommunication means as multimedia tools.

Multimedia tools can be practically any tools that can bring different types of information to learning and other educational activities. In this case, the notion of multimedia tools can also include outdated analog learning tools, which have become obsolete.

However, computers and their corresponding peripheral equipment are most often referred to as multimedia tools. However, in this section of the textbook, it makes sense to list the basic tools, the use of which in school allows teachers and students to deal not only with text or pictures, but also with audio, video or other direct information.

In different years, various means penetrated into school education, the emergence of which raised to a qualitatively new level the information support of the general secondary education system, which always had a positive impact on the effectiveness of training specialists.

At present, such technical means can be found in schools of the Republic of Kazakhstan:

- means for recording and reproduction of sound (electrophones, tape recorders, CB players),

- Telephone, telegraph and radio communication systems and facilities (telephone sets, fax machines, teletypes, telephone exchanges, radio communication systems),

- TV and radio broadcasting systems and facilities (TV and radio receivers, educational TV and radio, VUV players),

- optical and projection cinematographic and photographic equipment (cameras, movie cameras, diaprojectors, movie projectors, epidiascopes),

- printing, copying, duplicating and other equipment intended for documenting and reproducing information (rotaprints, photocopiers, rizographs, microfilming systems),

- computer facilities enabling electronic presentation, processing and storage of information (computers, printers, scanners, graphing machines),

Telecommunication systems providing information transmission via communication channels (modems, networks of wire, satellite, fiber-optic, radio relay and other types of communication channels designed for information transmission).

Technical means allow to bring to educational activities the possibility of operating with information of different types, such as sound, text, photo and video images. These tools, in some cases, turn out to be very complex in technical and technological terms and may well be considered as multimedia tools.

The computer, which has penetrated into the sphere of education, is a universal means of information processing. The computer's universality consists in the fact that, on the one hand, it alone is able to process information of different types (multimedia information), on the other hand, one and the same computer is able to perform a whole range of operations with information of the same type. Due to this fact, a computer together with an appropriate set of peripheral devices is able to provide all the functions of technical multimedia learning tools.

Regardless of make, model, time of creation, and application, all personal computers used in schooling share fundamental features, including:

1. Single-user operation, when only one person works with the computer at any given time. This does not exclude simultaneous execution of several information processing operations;

2. Ability to process, store, present and transmit information of different types, including text, numerical data, graphic images, sound and others (multimedia information);

3. Uniform communication with the user in a language close to natural communication;

4. Collaboration with various hardware multimedia devices that significantly expand the capabilities of a personal computer for processing, storing, presenting and transmitting information of various types;

5. Execution of information processing operations under the control of specially developed computer programs aimed both at maintaining the operation of various system functions of the computer and at solving applied tasks significant for the informatization of human activity.

Multimedia technologies allow many types of information to be integrated in a meaningful and harmonious way. It allows the computer to present information in various forms such as:

- images, including scanned photographs, drawings, maps and slides;

- voice recordings, sound effects and music;

- video, complex video effects;

- Animation and animation simulation.

Modern computer multimedia and multimedia technologies are closely related to the rapidly developing computer telecommunications. Practically all information resources published in computer networks are multimedia tools. And, on the contrary, the majority of multimedia tools and technologies, created nowadays, are oriented to work in telecommunication modes.

The wide introduction of telecommunication networks into all spheres of human life, including general secondary education, became possible only after the emergence of the global computer network Internet. The Internet is based on the ideas of standardization of information transfer protocols, openness of architecture and the possibility of free connection of new networks. All this, together, led to the spread of the Internet in different countries of the world, to the use of this telecommunication network in various spheres of human activity, including school education.

The use of telecommunication networks in school combined with the use of multimedia technologies and resources opens up new possibilities, the main ones being:

- increasing access to educational and methodological multimedia information;

- formation of students' communication skills, culture of communication, ability to search for multimedia information;

- organization of prompt advisory assistance;

- increasing individualization of learning, developing the basis for independent learning;

- providing virtual training sessions (seminars, lectures) in real time mode;

- organization of distance learning;

- organization of joint research projects;

- Modeling research activities;

- access to unique equipment, modeling of complex or hazardous objects, phenomena or processes, etc.;

- formation of a network community of teachers;

- formation of a network community of schoolchildren;

- development of critical thinking, skills of search and selection of reliable and necessary multimedia information.

Perhaps telecommunication multimedia tools used in general secondary education should be understood as any means and tools related to the transmission of multimedia information used in schools. With this approach, telecommunication tools used in education would include telephone, television and many other telecommunication devices in addition to computers and software. This definition has every right to exist.

But, at the same time, universal possibilities of telecommunication networks make it inexpedient to further penetration of all mentioned means of informatization into general secondary education. They simply lose their relevance. Telecommunication computer networks fully replace all other telecommunication means, possessing a whole range of additional possibilities. In this regard, it becomes justified to refer only computer means of transmitting educational multimedia information to the telecommunication means used in the sphere of education.

Thanks to the use of telecommunication means, well-known telecommunication services such as e-mail, teleconferences, remote access to information resources and others have penetrated into the sphere of education. All of them also allow working with multimedia information and are powerful tools that expand the scope of multimedia use in teaching schoolchildren.

§ 2.2 Specialized multimedia tools and their use in teaching.

As a rule, the majority of teachers and students, who are familiar with computer hardware in one way or another, unmistakably refer to acoustic systems (speakers), computer sound card (board), microphone, special computer video camera and, probably, joystick as multimedia hardware. All these devices, indeed, are common components of multimedia equipment, easy enough to use, have a fairly clear purpose and do not require any detailed description. Specialized multimedia tools, the main purpose of which is to increase the effectiveness of training, may be of much more interest. Interactive multimedia boards are among such modern tools, first of all.

The software and hardware set "Interactive whiteboard" is a modern multimedia tool, which, having all the qualities of a traditional blackboard, has wider possibilities of graphical commenting of screen images; allows to control and monitor the work of all students in the class at the same time; naturally (by increasing the flow of information) to increase the learning load of students in the classroom; to ensure ergonomic learning; to create new motivational prerequisites for learning; to conduct the learning process. The interactive whiteboard allows projecting the image from the monitor screen onto the projection board, as well as controlling the computer with special felt-tip pens, being constantly near the board, as it would be with a keyboard or a "mouse" manipulator.

The interactive whiteboard software used (SMART Board Software) includes the following tools:

- notebook (SMART Notebook);

- video recording tool (SMART Recorder);

- video player (SMART Video Player);

- additional (marker) tools (Floating Tools);

- virtual keyboard (SMART Keyboard).

All of these tools can be used separately or in combination depending on the learning objectives being addressed.

Notebook is a graphical editor that allows you to create documents of your own format and include text, graphical objects, both created in other Windows programs and with the help of appropriate tools.

The video recording tool allows you to record into a video file (AVI format) all manipulations currently performed on the board, and then play it back with a video player (SMART Player) or any other similar software. For example, using a notebook, you can draw a graph of a function or make a drawing, and then demonstrate the drawing process again by running the video file.

Additional (marker) tools are used to make various kinds of marks on the entire area of the monitor screen, regardless of the current application being used. All marks made by the teacher, e.g. in a Power Point presentation, can be saved.

The virtual keyboard is used to control the computer when the teacher is directly near the board, i.e. it duplicates the standard computer keyboard.

An important characteristic of the interactive whiteboard is its "dimensionlessness", i.e. the recorded information can be placed on an area of unlimited size, and everything that is recorded on the whiteboard can be stored indefinitely. All information displayed on the board can be used throughout the lesson. The teacher or student can go back to previous information at any time. In addition, all information from the current lesson can be used in subsequent lessons without requiring additional preparation.

Unlike the traditional whiteboard, the interactive whiteboard has more tools for graphical commenting of screen images, which allows to increase the quality of the image of the presented information to accentuate the attention of students, namely: more colors for the pen, different shapes and thickness of the pen, as well as the ability to set different colors of the background of the board. The interactive whiteboard allows saving time during the lesson when creating various drawings, schemes, diagrams, charts, graphs, as it has a large number of tools for drawing geometric figures.

Another feature of the interactive whiteboard is the ability to save the information recorded on it in the format of a video movie. For example, it is possible to record the solution of a problem in such a way that later you can view not a static final result, but the process of solving the problem from beginning to end, and at any speed.

The interactive whiteboard can be used as an effective means of creating educational and didactic materials: examples of problem solving, schemes, drawings, graphs, etc., both static and dynamic. All these materials can be created directly at the lesson, and can be further used when explaining new material, during repetition, and as simulators for individual work.

We can conditionally distinguish four properties of the interactive whiteboard, which determine all possible methods of its use:

- unlimited space,

- extended set of tools for capturing information and graphical commenting on screen images,

- possibility to save the recorded information in electronic form and its further unlimited replication,

- ability to save information in dynamic form (to a video file).

Let us illustrate these techniques using an example of a lesson in secondary school in the form of a talk or lecture. When teaching a lesson, the teacher fixes key points of his/her story on the blackboard as if he/she were doing it on a regular blackboard. This may be an example of problem solving, a brief definition of a concept, a drawing, a graph, etc. At the same time, he moves to a new screen (we will call it a slide) in case there is not enough space on the board. Each slide can be designed as a logically complete module. During the lesson, you can instantly return to previous slides to make additional notes or any changes. The number of slides is unlimited.

When the teacher writes on the board, he/she can choose almost any color of pen, as well as choose the thickness of the pen, i.e. each slide can be decorated in different colors and style at the discretion of the teacher for better clarity. The teacher may use static graphic images prepared in advance or taken from previous lessons in his/her story, and he/she may make various marks that are saved on the image used. These marks can be made with a pen or marker, whose properties (color, thickness, shape, transparency) can be customized. If the teacher uses a video clip in his lecture, he has the possibility to annotate the video image with the same tools, and in two modes, without stopping the video sequence or in pause mode. The possibility of saving the recorded information in electronic form allows the teacher to use it in the next lesson during repetition or in the future at the lessons of generalization of knowledge. Thus, the teacher prepares teaching material for the next lessons directly at the lesson.

The saved information can be given to students in electronic or paper form for independent work in class or at home. The information saved in the form of a video clip can be used in the lesson as a simulator at the stage of knowledge consolidation.

This way of saving learning material can be used to create demonstrations of examples of solving problems or performing tasks (finish a drawing, complete a figure or graph, etc.).

§ 2.3 Software tools for multimedia creation.

Teachers and pupils are not the developers of multimedia resources used in education. Most often, teachers and schoolchildren act as users of such tools. However, practice shows that every year more and more teachers cannot stay away from the development of even simple, but electronic learning tools. In this regard, it is advisable for a modern teacher to have an idea of both the technologies of developing high-quality multimedia resources and hardware and software tools - tools for creating computer-based learning tools.

Various HTML editors are widely used to create many simple multimedia resources. It should be taken into account that the HTML language is dynamically developing, so that resources that meet the new language standard may not be reproduced correctly by older versions of browsers.

In addition, the use of browsers for browsing imposes further constraints on the nature of the presentation of instructional multimedia information.

It should be noted that the programming systems used to create local components allow to include in the multimedia course and access to Internet resources, integrating network and local educational resources.

More specifically, it should be noted that the following languages and tools are most often used in the creation of multimedia hypertext resources and multimedia pages for the Internet:

- Hypertext Markup Language (HTML) is a standard language used on the Internet to create, format, and display information pages;

- Java is a specialized object-oriented programming language similar to C++. This language was developed specifically for the use of interactive graphics and animation in Internet resources. Many ready-made applications (Java applets) are available on the Internet and they can be downloaded to the user's computer for further use in creating their own information network and non-network multimedia resources;

VRML (Virtual Reality Modeling Language) allows you to create and place three-dimensional objects on the network that create the illusion of a real object much stronger than simple animations. Such three-dimensional objects are called "virtual rooms", "virtual galleries" and "worlds" depending on their "volume";

CGI (Common Gateway Interface) is not a programming language, but a specification describing the rules of information gathering and database creation. Developers use PERL or some other language in order to create CGI programs that allow to place in the network and provide the work of "dynamic documents". Thus, for example, users encounter such programs when filling in questionnaires and feedback forms in real time on Internet pages, answering test questions, etc.

Teachers and students can use other tools to create multimedia resources. To do this, educators must choose an editing program that will be used to create the pages of the multimedia resource. There are a variety of multimedia development tool environments available to create fully functional multimedia applications. Packages such as Macromedia Director or Authoware Professional are highly professional and expensive development tools, while FrontPage, mPower 4.0, HyperStudio 4.0 and Web Workshop Pro are their simpler and cheaper counterparts. Tools such as PowerPoint and text editors (e.g. Word) can also be used to create simple multimedia resources.

The listed development tools are provided with detailed documentation that is easy to read and understand. Of course, there are many other development tools that can be used with equal success in place of these.

Multimedia information posted on the Internet can be computer files of rather large size. This may be due to the presence of interactivity tools, audio and video fragments, high-resolution graphic images, etc., which can be used in the educational process. Due to insufficient bandwidth and reliability of existing communication channels, full-scale use of such information resources in the educational process may be difficult.

In some cases, problems related to the absence or poor quality of telecommunication networks can be avoided by working with such resources in local mode. In the course of local interaction with a multimedia resource, pupils receive information not from telecommunication networks, but from sources of internal or external memory of their own computer. At the same time, the content of the information resource and the ways of presenting information in it fully correspond to those posted on the Internet. Often, such resources are simply copied from network sources during a telecommunication session and then presented to students in a local version.

The relatively large volume of multimedia information provided in this case does not allow the use of traditional flexible magnetic disks (floppy disks) for its transfer and storage. Partially, the storage of a set of Internet sites can be provided by using non-removable hard magnetic disks ("hard disk drives"), available on all modern computers. However, this way of presenting multimedia information almost completely blocks the possibility of transferring information from one computer to another. The most promising, from the point of view of education, means of storing multimedia information obtained from the Internet are optical laser CDs (OLCs). Due to high-tech laser methods of recording and reading information on this medium with its relatively small physical size, it is possible to qualitatively present quite a large amount of multimedia information.

Using O) as a learning tool can bring the following key benefits to the school's learning process:

▪ providing schoolchildren with multimedia information, traditionally placed on telecommunication means, taking into account its structure and specifics of visualization;

▪ providing learners with new opportunities for deep understanding of course content and its interrelationships, training of skills and abilities, memorization and self-control of knowledge;

▪ compensation for insufficient time devoted by the teacher to individual work with the student and, in some cases, insufficient professionalism of the Teacher;

▪ realization of integrated multimedia impact with feedback;

▪ Ensuring self-monitoring within a time constraint;

High mobility, portability and replicability of multimedia information material used in the educational process.

The issues of multimedia resources development for general secondary education are multidimensional and not simple. Technical and technological peculiarities of such developments are considered in special literature. The main issues of content and ergonomic problems concerning the creation of multimedia resources will be partially discussed in other subsections of this manual.

Chapter 3.

Information multimedia resources
§ 3.1 Educational multimedia resources. Classification of multimedia resources and their components

The introduction of multimedia resources into the educational process of the school takes place in accordance with two main directions.

Educational multimedia resources, introduced according to the first direction, are included in the educational process as "supporting" tools within the framework of traditional methods of the historically established system of general secondary education. In this case, information resources act as a means of intensifying the learning process, individualization of learning and partial automation of teachers' routine work related to accounting, control and assessment of students' knowledge.

The second direction of introduction of multimedia resources is a more complex process leading to changes in the content of education, revision of methods and forms of organization of the educational process, construction of holistic courses based on the use of the content of information sources in individual school disciplines.

In this case, we are talking about the fact that the basis for the creation, description, classification and application of multimedia resources should be the psychological principle of activity and the psychological principle of "cultivation".

According to the first principle, the development of the student is based on the active appropriation by him/her, with the help of the teacher, of social-historical ways of activity or means of communication. In this case, teaching acts as an organization of conditions for the appropriation by pupils of these or those forms of communication and activity. In the course of realization of this principle it is possible to introduce multimedia resources in both the first and the second directions.

According to the second principle, the dual nature of pedagogical influence is recognized. On the one hand, realizing the social order, the teacher manages the formation of personality, on the other hand, the management is based on the teacher's conscious consideration of individual qualities of students. "Cultivation" of the pupil's personality takes place in the conditions of organization of self-determination of the latter, with maximum awareness of the nature of the learned activity (only in this case he considers it "his"). When the student's change in general remains subjectively selfchanging, the teacher can only contribute to the desired change by creating "natural conditions" through communication with the student. In this case, knowledge is "given" to the student under the need formed in the process of previous learning communication. The introduction of multimedia resources during the realization of this principle is carried out according to the second direction described above.

These principles are most adequately and fully reflected in the person-centered learning model. Its goal is to promote the development of the learner as a person, to form his/her needs in self-education and self-determination in learning and life situations with the awareness of personal responsibility. Knowledge, skills and abilities in this model are considered not as a goal, but as a means of personal development of the learner, which generates specific needs of the education system in information sources.

The main types of educational electronic information resources that can be based on the use of multimedia technologies are:

- information retrieval and reference multimedia systems,

- applied multimedia encyclopedias,

- multimedia tools to control and measure the level of knowledge, skills and abilities of schoolchildren,

- electronic simulators,

- Multimedia tools for mathematical and simulation modeling,

- Multimedia tools for remote access laboratories and virtual laboratories,

- automated training systems,

- electronic multimedia textbooks,

- expert training systems,

- intelligent tutoring systems.

This enumeration defines a description of the main groups of all possible multimedia resources. Each of the possible standard types of multimedia resources falls under one of the following descriptions.

Information retrieval and reference multimedia systems are designed for entering, storing, searching and presenting information to teachers, students and parents. Such systems can include various hypermedia programs that provide hierarchical organization of material and quick search of multimedia information by one or another feature. Databases of all kinds are also widely used. Database management systems provide the ability to search and sort multimedia information. Databases can be used in the educational process of school to organize the presentation of the content of educational material and its analysis. Modern educational process needs specialized educational databases adapted for independent work of schoolchildren in order to search and analyze the necessary information.

From the concept of information retrieval system directly follows the more modern and widespread in connection with the expansion of telecommunication systems and portals the concept of applied multimedia encyclopedia, which is a set of educational information modules together with the corresponding management system. Applied multimedia encyclopedias give rise to one of the most common forms for the development of educational multimedia resources.

An applied multimedia encyclopedia can correspond to one school discipline or a group of disciplines. In this case, an educational module can be dedicated to a certain topic or concept considered in the academic disciplines. For example, the module may contain material corresponding to the content of only one paragraph of a traditional school textbook or describe a concept used in teaching several general education disciplines at once.

Today's variable learning system requires multimedia encyclopedias that provide several alternative modules for each topic or concept in order to ensure adaptability to different learning environments. The modules should be differentiated by their focus on different groups of teachers or students, methodological features, detail and style of presentation, references to different examples, etc.

Improvement of the encyclopedia consists in the development and addition of new modules, correction or elimination of outdated material, and development of the management system. At the same time, improvement is possible not only by a predetermined circle of authors or specialists in a given subject area, but also by ordinary teachers who create their own versions of multimedia resources. In practice, such expansion of encyclopedias takes place locally on the computers of specific teachers and schoolchildren or directly at the place of encyclopedia publication with the help of telecommunication means.

The management system of the applied multimedia encyclopedia performs such functions as version management of the information multimedia resource, maintenance of dictionaries, management of hyperlinks, harmonization of data formats, replacement of terms with synonyms and symbols of values with recommended symbols for the uniformity of naming concepts within the version of one resource, registration of modules, providing the interface in a language close to natural, etc.

The basis for creation and classification of an applied electronic encyclopedia is knowledge structuring, allocation of subject area concepts and relations between them. All this is the basis for building a structured knowledge management system of the encyclopedia and is used to unify module interfaces when developing versions of this multimedia resource.

Multimedia tools for controlling and measuring schoolchildren's knowledge level are widely represented in telecommunication environments and are widely used in general secondary education due to their relative ease of creation. There is a whole range of instrumental systems-shells with the help of which a teacher, even if he/she is not familiar with the basics of programming, is able to compose lists of questions and possible answers on one or another topic of the school program. As a rule, the student's task is to choose one correct answer from a number of suggested answers.

The need of the school education system for such multimedia resources is conditioned by the necessity to relieve teachers from the routine work of issuing individual control tasks and checking the correctness of their fulfillment. This is especially relevant in the conditions of mass school training and the need to correlate learning outcomes with the requirements of state educational standards.

Multiple and more frequent control of knowledge, including self-control, stimulates repetition and, accordingly, consolidation of learning material.

Electronic simulators are designed for practicing practical skills and abilities. Such multimedia resources are required in the educational process for training in complex and even emergency situations when practicing emergency response, when the use of real installations for training is undesirable for a number of reasons (possibility of creating emergency situations, increased danger, etc.). In addition, electronic simulators are used for practicing problem-solving skills. In this case, they provide brief information on theory, training at different levels of independence, control and self-control.

Multimedia tools for mathematical and simulation modeling can also be considered as educational multimedia resources, due to the fact that they allow to expand the boundaries of experimental and theoretical research, to supplement the physical experiment with a computational experiment, to provide schoolchildren and teachers with additional information data. In some cases, such resources are used to model objects of research, in other cases - measuring installations. The system of general secondary education needs prompt access to such multimedia resources in order to reduce the cost of purchasing expensive laboratory equipment and to reduce the level of safety of work in educational laboratories. Modeling multimedia tools can also include subject-oriented software environments that provide the ability to operate models-objects of a certain class.

Automated training systems, as a rule, are training multimedia resources of relatively small volume. Such multimedia resources provide familiarization of students with theoretical material, training and control of knowledge level.

Electronic multimedia textbooks along with multimedia encyclopedias are the main educational multimedia resources. EI are created at a high scientific and methodological level and should fully comply with the discipline component of the educational standard of general secondary education. In addition, multimedia textbooks should ensure the continuity and completeness of the didactic cycle of the learning process under the condition of interactive feedback.

School practice shows that the use of electronic copies of traditional "paper" textbooks in the educational process does not lead to an increase in the effectiveness of learning, but, on the contrary, is sometimes a significant negative factor in relation to the use of conventional printed publications. In this connection, one of the main requirements for multimedia textbooks, which are put forward taking into account the needs of the educational process, is that the reduction of such a textbook to the "paper" version (printing out the content) should always lead to the loss of specific didactic properties inherent in a multimedia textbook.

Expert learning systems are realized on the basis of ideas and technologies of artificial intelligence. Such multimedia resources model the activity of experts in solving rather complex tasks and are capable of acquiring new knowledge, providing an answer to the learner's request, as well as solving problems from a certain subject area of school education. At the same time, expert training systems based on multimedia technologies provide explanation of strategies and tactics of problem solving in the course of dialog support of the solution process. Unfortunately, when working with such systems, such links of the didactic cycle of the schoolchildren's learning process as the organization of students' application of the acquired primary knowledge and receiving feedback (control of students' actions) are not realized. When working with expert learning systems, students do not have to search for a solution themselves, and, accordingly, such a link of the didactic cycle as receiving feedback is not realized.

Intelligent learning systems are educational multimedia resources of the highest level and are also realized on the basis of artificial intelligence ideas. Such resources can control all stages of solving a learning task, starting from its formulation and search for the solution principle and ending with the assessment of the solution optimality, taking into account the peculiarities of schoolchildren's activity. Such multimedia resources provide dialog interaction, as a rule, in a language close to natural language.

The modern system of general secondary education is in need of intelligent learning systems, in the course of the educational dialog with which not only the correctness of certain actions, but also the strategy of searching for a solution, planning of actions, methods of control, etc. could be discussed. In such systems, reflexive learning management should be carried out on the basis of the learner's model (refined in the course of the learning process). Multimedia resources should improve the learning strategy as data are accumulated. A distinctive feature of intelligent training systems is that they do not contain the main and auxiliary training effects in a ready-made form, but generate them.

§ 3.2 Interactivity and modeling

Modern educational multimedia resources used in teaching schoolchildren are not limited to simple presentation of material. All of them, as a rule, interact with the student - they ask him/her questions, offer to participate in the course of events taking place on the computer screen, choose the trajectory of learning the material. There is a dialog between the student and the computer. The presence of such properties in a multimedia resource is called interactivity.

We will define interactivity more precisely a little later, but for now let us consider in detail the properties of a dialog that can occur in a schoolchild or a teacher with a computer and an interactive multimedia resource running on it.

It should be taken into account that the interaction of a learner with any multimedia resource is not a dialog in the full sense of the word. According to one of the existing definitions, dialog is the development of a topic, position, point of view by the joint efforts of two or more people who are in interaction and communication about a certain or unknown in some details content. In this regard, the process of communication of a schoolchild or a teacher with a multimedia resource, which in many respects overlaps with human-to-human communication, is also commonly referred to as dialog.

In the opinion of some teachers, there can be no real dialogue with a computer, or, more precisely, with an array of formalized multimedia information. What is called "dialog mode" from the didactic point of view is only a variation of either the sequence or the amount of multimedia information given. These procedures are probably the end of the possibilities of operating with ready-made, fixed in memory machine information of various types.

Dialogue is the objective dialectical contradiction of the subject realized in pedagogical communication, and even the most modern machine cannot master the contradiction, it is not fundamentally adapted to it. It evaluates the introduction of contradictory information as unsatisfactory.

This means that modern educational multimedia resources do not provide creative processes even when they carry out educational simulation modeling, set the mode of "intellectual game", despite the fact that it is in this form of learning that the use of computers and multimedia is most promising. Such resources help teachers to create such a learning environment, which does not predetermine the formation of students' thinking, but promotes such formation.

In the process of a student's work with a multimedia resource, the personal regulation of thinking activity changes: the role of personal defense mechanisms increases, the subjective level of goal attainability increases, activity control mechanisms are reorganized, and motivation is transformed. The impact on the motivational sphere allows to manage the goal education. It can be assumed that there is a new form of communication between the participants of the educational process, mediated by the use of the latest means of information and telecommunication technologies in education.

The interactivity of multimedia resources used in the education system means that the student is given the opportunity to actively interact with such media.

It should be noted that dialog is most often understood as an exchange of information involving two parties. In science, there is a broader understanding of dialog, and its main feature is not the exchange of speech messages of interlocutors, but the presence of several positions.

When working with educational multimedia resources, a single level of interaction, corresponding to a dialog between a teacher and one student, can be considered optimal.

The main psychological factors that characterize dialogue include:

- general psychological principles of dialog construction,

- organization of the communication process,

- linguistic aspects (choice of the language of communication, construction of the text of the message, its shape, size, etc.),

- communication modality (type of information presentation and trainees' responses),

- meaningful aspects of communication.

In case of using correct approaches to the creation of multimedia resources, they model not just communication, but pedagogical communication, which creates conditions for the development of motivation and the correct formation of the personality of the schoolchild, provides a favorable emotional climate of learning at school.

At the same time, an important prerequisite for an effective dialog between a schoolchild and a multimedia resource is the observance of social distance. It is known that the reduction of this distance, which is usually expressed in familiaristic treatment of the interlocutor, leads to the loss of the teacher's authority in the learning environment. In the practice of informatized learning, this shortcoming is expressed in the use of "on you", in the abuse of humor, as a result of which the learners may have a desire to put the learning tool in a deadlock. The same desire appears in students when the social distance is unreasonably large, when the computer's remarks are given in a categorical form that hurts the ego of students.

The greatest importance should be given to the pedagogical orientation of the dialog, i.e. the focus on achieving learning objectives. Another essential requirement for the dialog between the learner and the multimedia tool should be the requirement of simplicity and minimum time for inputting the answer. It is necessary to construct the dialog in such a way that the learners think about the content of their answer, not about how to enter it into the computer.

To ensure flexibility and clarity of the learner's dialogue with the multimedia resource, a rational organization of the user interface is necessary.

Thus, dialog is an essential component of the interactivity discussed at the beginning of the subsection.

There are three main types of interactivity used by educational multimedia tools:

- Reactive interaction: learners show a response to situations presented to them.

The sequence of tasks is rigidly fixed and there are few opportunities to control the multimedia program;

- active interaction: students control the multimedia resource. Students decide in which order to perform the tasks and which path of learning to follow within the multimedia resource;

- two-way interaction: learners and multimedia resources can mutually adapt to each other.

Multimedia interactivity implies a wide range of opportunities for teachers and students to influence the learning process and content, including:

- manipulating on-screen objects;

- linear navigation - scrolling within the screen;

- hierarchical navigation - selection of meaningful subsections using a hierarchically organized menu system;

- interactive help function called by special buttons on the navigation bar. Context-sensitive help is the most effective;

- User interaction, where the tool has the ability to respond to teacher or student requests and actions;

- constructive interaction, when a multimedia resource provides the ability to create or configure screen objects;

- reflective interaction, when the multimedia resource takes into account the user's actions for subsequent analysis (for example, in order to recommend to the student the optimal sequence of studying the material on the basis of this information), the choice between "expert" or "introductory" variant of studying;

- simulative interactivity in the case when screen objects are connected with each other and interact in such a way that the setting of these objects determines their "behavior" (simulating the real functioning of technical devices, social processes, etc.);

- In-depth contextual interactivity, through which the learner is involved in various activities that have an implicit didactic value. This type of interactivity is used in numerous entertaining and educational multimedia programs and in various multimedia games for schoolchildren;

- in-depth contextual interactivity, reduced to the specifics of functioning of virtual reality systems, in which students and the Teacher are immersed in a simulated three-dimensional world.

Closely related to the concept of interactivity is the concept of modeling. Many multimedia resources are modeling.

Modeling multimedia resources make it possible to expand the boundaries of experimental and theoretical research, to supplement the physical experiment with a computational experiment, to provide schoolchildren and teachers with additional information data. In some cases, such resources are used to model objects of research, in other cases - measuring installations. The modeling multimedia tools can also include subject-oriented software environments that provide the ability to operate models-objects.

Speaking about computer modeling, it should be noted that nowadays, when introducing multimedia technologies in the educational process, it is necessary to focus on the creation of generalized information models of entire classes of technical objects (then this or that real technical device will be perceived as a private implementation) and on the creation of all kinds of simulation laboratory models, simulators, including virtual models.

Computer models, as a rule, are not universal. Each of them is designed to simulate a rather narrow range of phenomena. Based on the technology of mathematical modeling, computer multimedia models can be used not only to demonstrate phenomena that are difficult to reproduce in a classroom environment, but also to interactively clarify the degree of influence of certain parameters on the simulated situation. This property allows using the models as simulators of laboratory installations, as well as for practicing the skills of controlling the modeled processes. Modern multimedia tools allow not only to work with ready-made models of objects, but also to construct them from individual elements.

§ 3.3 Quality of educational multimedia resources. The system of requirements for the quality of multimedia resources

The general secondary education system has a significant need for quality multimedia resources, which in practice would allow:

- to organize various forms of pupils' activity on independent extraction and presentation of knowledge;

- apply the full range of possibilities of modern information and telecommunication technologies in the process of performing various types of learning activities, including such as registration, collection, storage, information processing, interactive dialog, modeling of objects, phenomena,   processes, functioning of laboratories (virtual, with remote access to real equipment), etc.;

- to bring direct information into the educational process along with associative information through the use of multimedia technologies, virtual reality, hypermedia systems;

- objectively diagnose and evaluate the intellectual capabilities of pupils, as well as the level of their knowledge, skills, abilities, skills, the level of preparation for a particular lesson in the disciplines of general education, to measure the results of mastering the material in accordance with the requirements of the state educational standard;

- manage the learning activity of schoolchildren adequately to the intellectual level of a particular student, the level of his/her knowledge, skills, abilities, peculiarities of his/her motivation, taking into account the implemented methods and used means of teaching;

- to create conditions for individual independent learning activities of students, to form skills of self-learning, self-development, self-improvement, self-education, self-realization;

- promptly provide teachers, students and parents with relevant, timely information that is consistent with the goals and content of general secondary education;

- create a framework for ongoing and responsive communication between teachers, learners and parents aimed at enhancing learning.

All, without exception, multimedia resources used in the system of general secondary education should meet the didactic requirements for traditional educational publications, such as textbooks, teaching and methodological manuals. Didactic requirements correspond to the needs of the educational process of the school and, accordingly, to the didactic principles of teaching. Standard didactic requirements for multimedia resources are discussed below.

The requirement to ensure the scientificity of teaching using multimedia resources means sufficient depth, correctness and scientific reliability of the presentation of the content of educational material provided by the resource, taking into account the latest scientific achievements. In accordance with the needs of the general secondary education system, the process of learning educational material with the help of multimedia resources should be based on the main methods of scientific knowledge: experiment, comparison, observation, abstraction,

generalization, concretization, analogy, induction and deduction, analysis and synthesis, modeling and system analysis.

The requirement to ensure the accessibility of education using multimedia resources means the need to determine the degree of theoretical complexity and depth of study of educational material in accordance with the age and individual characteristics of schoolchildren. It is inadmissible to overcomplicate and overload the educational material, when mastering this material becomes impossible for the learner.

The requirement to provide problem-based learning is conditioned by the essence and nature of learning and cognitive activity. When a schoolchild faces a problematic situation that needs to be solved, his/her thinking activity increases. The level of fulfillment of this didactic requirement with the help of multimedia resources can be much higher than when using traditional textbooks and manuals.

The requirement to ensure the visualization of learning means the need to take into account the sensual perception of the studied objects, their models or models and their personal observation by the student. The requirement of visualization in the case of using multimedia resources should be realized at a fundamentally new, higher level. The spread of virtual reality systems will allow in the near future to speak not only about visibility, but also about polysensory learning.

The requirement to ensure consciousness of learning, independence and activation of the learner's activity presupposes that multimedia tools provide students with independent actions to extract educational information with a clear understanding of the ultimate goals and objectives of learning activity. At the same time, the content, to which the student's learning activity is directed, is realized for the student. The functioning and use of multimedia resources should be based on the activity approach. Therefore, a clear model of the learner's activity should be traced in the corresponding resources. The motives of his/her activity should be adequate to the content of the learning material. To increase the activity of learning, the subsystems of multimedia resources should generate learning situations, formulate questions, provide students with the opportunity to choose one or another learning path, the ability to control the course of events.

The requirement to ensure the systematicity and consistency of learning when using multimedia resources means ensuring the need of the learning system to ensure that students consistently master a certain system of knowledge in the studied subject area, the need for knowledge, skills and abilities to be formed in a certain system, in a logically justified order. This requires:

- presentation of educational material in a systematized and structured form;

- taking into account both the retrospective and prospective of the knowledge, skills and abilities being formed when forming and presenting each portion of learning information;

- taking into account the interdisciplinary connections of the material studied;

- didactically substantiated sequence of teaching material presentation and teaching influences;

- organization of the process of knowledge acquisition in a sequence determined by the logic of learning;

- ensuring the connection between the information provided by the multimedia resource and practice by selecting examples, creating meaningful game moments, presenting practical tasks, experiments, models of real processes and phenomena.

The requirement to ensure the unity of educational, developmental and educational functions of teaching when using multimedia resources.

The requirement to ensure the content and functional validity of test and measurement subsystems of multimedia resources. The needs of the teaching system impose on such resources the requirements to ensure the compliance of the control and measurement material with the content of the teaching material (content validity) and the assessed level of pupils' activity (functional validity).

The requirement to ensure reliability in the use of control and measurement subsystems of multimedia resources is defined as the probability of correct measurement of the level of learning of educational material using multimedia resources. The requirement meets the needs of the general secondary education system in ensuring the sustainability of the results of repeated measurement or control of learning outcomes of the same pupil.

In addition to the traditional didactic requirements for multimedia resources and traditional educational publications, multimedia resources should also have specific didactic requirements due to the existing needs of the school teaching system and the use of modern information and telecommunication technologies in the creation and functioning of multimedia resources.

The requirement of adaptability implies the adaptability of educational multimedia resources to individual capabilities of a schoolchild. The requirement means adaptation, adaptation of the learning process using multimedia resources to the level of knowledge and skills, psychological peculiarities of the learner. It is reasonable to distinguish three levels of resource adaptation. The first level of adaptation is the possibility for the learner to choose the most suitable for him/her individual pace of learning the material. The second level of adaptation implies the diagnosis of the learner's condition, based on the results of which the content and methods of training are proposed. The third level of adaptation is based on an open approach, which does not imply classification of possible users and consists in the fact that the authors of a multimedia resource strive to develop as many variants of its use for as many schoolchildren as possible.

The requirement of interactivity of learning means that in the learning process there should be a two-way interaction of a schoolchild with educational multimedia resources. Such tools should provide dialog and feedback. An important part of the dialog organization is the obligatory adequate response of multimedia resources to the action of teachers and students. Feedback tools control and correct student's actions, give recommendations for further work, and provide constant access to reference and explanatory information. In case of control with diagnostics of errors based on the results of learning work, feedback tools provide the results of work analysis with recommendations to improve the level of knowledge.

The requirement to develop the intellectual potential of the learner when working with multimedia resources meets the needs of the general secondary education system to form the students' thinking styles (algorithmic, visual and figurative, theoretical), the ability to make an optimal decision or variant decisions in a complex situation, the ability to process information (based on the use of data processing systems, information retrieval systems, databases, etc.).

The requirement of systematic and structural-functional connectedness of presentation of educational material in multimedia resources.

The requirement to ensure the formability and uniqueness of tasks in the control and measurement subsystems of multimedia resources. According to this requirement, the tasks presented to schoolchildren should not fully exist before the beginning of measurement or control and should be formed randomly at the moment of the student's work with multimedia resources. At the same time, the tasks received by different students should be different, which meets the needs of education in ensuring objectivity and adequacy of pedagogical measurements.

The requirement to ensure the completeness (integrity) and continuity of the didactic cycle of learning using multimedia resources means that such resources should provide an opportunity to perform all links of the didactic cycle within one session of work with information and telecommunication technology.

The didactic requirements for multimedia resources are closely related to methodological requirements. Methodological requirements imply taking into account the needs of teaching a particular school discipline, the specifics of the corresponding science, its conceptual apparatus, peculiarities of research methods of its regularities; possibilities of realization of modern methods of information processing and methodology of educational activity realization.

Multimedia resources should meet the following methodological requirements.

Due to the diversity of real technical systems and devices, as well as due to the complexity of their functioning, the presentation of educational material using multimedia resources should be based on the interrelation and interaction of conceptual, figurative and action components of students' thinking.

Multimedia resources should ensure the reflection of the system of scientific concepts of a school discipline in the form of a hierarchical structure, each level of which corresponds to a certain intradisciplinary level of abstraction, as well as to ensure the consideration of both single-level and inter-level logical interrelationships of these concepts. Such an approach contributes to meeting the need of learning systems in effective methods of presenting educational material due to the possibility of sequential traversal of the hierarchical structure and explanation of scientific concepts of the educational field.

Educational multimedia resources should provide schoolchildren with the opportunity to perform controlled training actions in order to gradually increase the intra-disciplinary level of knowledge abstraction at the level of assimilation sufficient for the implementation of algorithmic and heuristic activities.

Along with taking into account didactic requirements for the development and use of multimedia resources, it is necessary to comply with a set of psychological requirements affecting the effectiveness of learning at school. The following psychological requirements are among the requirements for all multimedia resources without exception.

The presentation of educational material in multimedia resources should correspond not only to verbal-logical, but also to sensory-perceptual and representational levels of cognitive process. Мультимедиа-ресурсы должны создаваться и функционировать с учетом особенностей таких познавательных психических процессов, как восприятие (преимущественно зрительное, а также слуховое, осязательное), внимание (его устойчивость, концентрация, переключаемость, распределение и объем внимания), мышление (теоретическое понятийное, теоретическое образное, практическое наглядно-образное, практическое наглядно-действенное), воображение, память (мгновенная, кратковременная, оперативная, долговременная, явление замещения информации в кратковременной памя

The presentation of educational material using multimedia resources should be oriented to the thesaurus and linguistic composition of a particular age contingent and the specifics of the students' training. Multimedia resources should be created and function taking into account pupils' knowledge system and language skills. The presentation of educational material should be understandable to a specific age contingent of learners, but should not be too simple, as it can lead to a decrease in attention.

The use of multimedia resources should be aimed at developing both figurative and logical thinking in pupils.

Ergonomic requirements for multimedia resources take into account the age characteristics of schoolchildren, provide an increase in the level of motivation for learning, set the requirements for the image of information and modes of operation of multimedia resources. The main ergonomic requirement is the requirement to ensure a humane attitude to the student, to organize a friendly interface in multimedia resources, to provide the possibility for students to use the necessary hints and methodological instructions, free sequence and pace of work, which will avoid negative impact on the psyche, create a benevolent atmosphere at school lessons.

Health-saving requirements for the development and use of multimedia resources correspond to hygiene requirements and sanitary norms for students' work with computer equipment. Multimedia resources should be developed and used in such a way that the time spent by a student working with the resource does not exceed the sanitary norms of working with the corresponding computer equipment. Failure to meet these requirements will result either in students not perceiving part of the multimedia information (in the case of age-specific requirements) or in the deterioration of health (sanitary and hygienic requirements).

With the penetration of multimedia resources into the educational process of schools in the system of general secondary education, the need for quality documentation accompanying multimedia resources increases. The requirements to the design of documentation for multimedia resources justify the need to check the correctness, completeness and detail of the design of methodological guidelines and instructions for users.

The creation and use of multimedia resources should be accompanied by appropriate documentation in order to provide an interface between developers , customers, teachers and students, as well as to ensure the possibility of learning and improving the functions of the multimedia resource. The documentation of the resources should be complete and ensure that they can be used effectively for student learning.

The documentation of multimedia resources should facilitate mobility, reuse and re-use of their components.

Chapter 4.

Internet multimedia resources.

§ 4.1 Remote access to multimedia resources. The Internet and its services.

The main source of multimedia resources for most teachers and schoolchildren is the World Wide Web. This network provides access to both educational and many other resources containing information of various types, ranging from text to complex video images. Nowadays, multimedia and hypermedia technologies are becoming inseparable from telecommunication technologies, and the World Wide Web is becoming a large and well-structured repository of multimedia information.

One of the most popular and promising services of network technologies related to multimedia is WWW-technology, which is a distributed system of hypermedia resources, the distinctive feature of which, in addition to an attractive appearance, is the ability to organize cross-references to each other. Using a special program for viewing WWW documents (browser), a network user can quickly navigate through links from one document to another, traveling through the space of the World Wide Web.

The most widespread communication technology and corresponding service in computer networks has become the technology of forwarding and processing of information messages, providing operational communication between people. Electronic mail (E-mail) is a system for storing and forwarding messages between people who have access to a computer network. E-mail can be used to transmit any multimedia information (text documents, images, digital data, sound recordings, etc.) over computer networks.

Such a service realizes:

- editing documents before transmission,

- storage of documents and messages,

- mail forwarding,

- checking and correcting errors that occur during transmission,

- issuing a confirmation of receipt of correspondence by the addressee,

- receiving and storing multimedia information,

- reviewing correspondence received.

E-mail can be used for non-verbal communication between participants of the educational process and sending multimedia (teaching and learning materials). To use e-mail, it is enough to learn a few commands of the e-mail client to send, receive and process information.

E-mail can be used by teachers for consultation, sending students' test papers and professional communication with colleagues. It is also advisable to use it to conduct electronic classes in asynchronous mode, when students are sent multimedia teaching material, excerpts from recommended literature, etc. in electronic form beforehand, and then consultations are conducted via e-mail.

Let's highlight the main possibilities of using e-mail in the educational process of the school:

- distribution of teaching materials to schoolchildren;

- organizing counseling;

- mutual learning in the exchange of information between pupils;

- conducting off-line distance lessons;

- communication between teachers and school administrators and parents of schoolchildren.

A distinctive feature and convenience of e-mail is the ability to send the same message to a large number of recipients at once.

A similar mailing principle is used by an Internet service called mailing lists. This service works in subscription mode. By subscribing to a mailing list, a teacher or schoolchild will receive a selection of e-mail messages on a selected topic at regular intervals. Mailing lists serve as periodicals on the Internet.

From a didactic point of view, mailing lists can be used to organize so-called "virtual training classes". The rules and methods of subscription are explained to the created study group and it starts working. Every message sent to the discussion group by any of its members is automatically distributed by the mailing list server to all participants. One of the participants (moderator) is the teacher.

The main didactic possibilities of using mailing lists are automatic distribution of teaching materials and organization of virtual classrooms.

Another **popular service** provided by modern telecommunication networks and realizing the exchange of multimedia information between people united by common interests is teleconferencing.

A teleconference is an online forum organized for discussion and messaging on a specific topic.

Teleconferencing allows you to post messages of interest on special computers on the network. The messages can be read by connecting to the computer and selecting a topic for discussion. Then, if desired, you can reply to the author of the article or send your own message. In this way, an online discussion with a newsworthy character is organized, since the messages are stored for a short period of time.

The availability of hardware multimedia means: audio and video equipment (microphone, digital video camera, etc.) connected to a computer allows organizing computer-based audio and video conferences, increasingly widespread in the system of general secondary education.

Unlike e-mail-based mailing lists, some teleconferences and newsgroups operate in real time. The difference is that in the case of a mailing list, information is exchanged off-line by automatic e-mail distribution. A news server publishes all messages on a shared board immediately, and stores them for some time. Thus, teleconferences allow organizing a discussion both in online and delayed mode. When organizing training sessions, it is advisable to use newsgroups moderated by the teacher.

One of the forms of conducting e-lessons using telecommunication multimedia technologies is the classic "question-and-answer" scenario. The teacher informs students in advance about the topic and questions of the seminar, then sets the time of the session. During the seminar, the teacher asks a question in writing to any student, who must answer it. A discussion of the answer can then be organized, or comments can be made. The results of the discussion are recorded, and at the end of the lesson the teacher can evaluate both the pupils' answers and their activity.

With the development of technical means of computer networks, the speed of data transmission is increasing. This allows users connected to the network not only to exchange text messages, but also to transmit multimedia resources such as sound and video images over a considerable distance. One of the representatives of programs that implement communication through the network is the program NetMeeting, which is part of the Internet Explorer suite. NetMeeting is a multimedia tool that realizes the possibilities of direct communication via the Internet.

It should be noted that to realize audio communication, you need appropriate multimedia hardware: sound card, microphone and loudspeakers. Video communication requires a video board and a camera, or only a camera that supports the Video for Windows standard.

The main areas of using NetMeeting in the middle school classroom are:

- organization of virtual lessons and consultations in real time, including voice communication and transmission of video images of teachers and students;

- exchange of information in text, graphic and sound modes;

- organization of joint work with educational information in on-line mode;

- sending educational and methodological information in the form of files in real time;

- interactive communication of teachers and administration with parents of

schoolchildren, in the future - telecommunication operational parent meetings.

Automated search of multimedia information is an important service realized in computer networks from the point of view of improving the efficiency of school education. Using specialized tools - information retrieval systems - it is possible to find information and multimedia resources of interest in the world information sources in the shortest possible time.

The use of modern telecommunication technologies allows not only to provide distributed in space and time access to educational information resources to all participants of the educational process, but also to involve in the formation of the content of multimedia resources and the system of educational portals both a large number of specialists and a large number of resources themselves.

In this regard, the development, layout, and cataloging of multimedia resources should take into account a system of organizational and technological provisions that are essential from the point of view of including links to multimedia resources in educational portals. Such a system should include several such basic technological constraints related to the development and functioning of multimedia resources:

1. The software included in the multimedia resource should be modular, which would allow to dynamically build up the multimedia resource remotely or use it in parts.

2. The multimedia resource should have the property of scalability, which will maximally simplify the process of its adaptation to the specifications of the educational portal and technological features of hardware and software of users working with the resource and the portal.

3. Multimedia resources should be adapted to work on telecommunication servers used by portal developers, specialists forming multimedia resources, developers of other resources included in the portal.

§ 4.2 Use of telecommunication multimedia resources in teaching schoolchildren

Most of the most qualitative multimedia resources, the use of which would increase the efficiency of general secondary education, are cataloged on educational Internet portals. At present, an organizational scheme for creating a system of educational portals, which has its own peculiarities, has already been developed. The organizational scheme of creating a system of educational portals includes:

- horizontal portal;

- profile vertical portals by fields of knowledge: humanitarian, economic and social,

natural-scientific, engineering, pedagogical, medical, agricultural etc;

- specialized vertical portals: book publishing, unified exam, education news, etc.

The horizontal gantry provides:

- to navigate all vertical portals;

- search for multimedia information in the field of education on the Internet;

- personalization and personal adaptation of the interface both by selecting the user's own category (learner, teacher, administrator, portal developer) and specifying the level of education, and by designing their own interface;

- formation and provision of slices of vertical portals by education levels;

- storage and provision of information in the field of education (legislation, orders, normative documents, standards, lists of specialties, federal set of textbooks, database of universities, etc.);

- publication of a daily press review of education issues;

- education news feed;
- organizing forums, discussion groups, mailing lists.

Profile vertical portals should contain materials for all levels of education: elementary school, secondary school, primary vocational education, secondary vocational education, higher education, additional education, postgraduate education.

Specialized vertical portals should provide information support and services for solving specific special tasks of all-Russian level. All vertical portals should have a common interface, common rules of updating and maintenance. Vertical portals will be able to fully use the reference information located on the upper horizontal portal, its search engine, means of personalization and adaptation of the interface.

The use of multimedia resources published on the Internet and cataloged on educational portals will not have a proper effect in general secondary education without determining the methods of using the resources in teaching schoolchildren.

The methods include the so-called project method - a special case of integrated learning technology. In the process of its implementation, such new forms of organizing learning activities as:

- students working in groups with network partners;
- assimilation of general cultural knowledge, formation of schoolchildren's worldview on the basis of multimedia information received by them through telecommunication channels;
- use of the latest multimedia technologies;
- The development of communicative writing in schoolchildren.

In addition, the use of such pedagogical technologies contributes to the organization of joint work of several teachers, the integration of curricular and extracurricular forms of work, changes in the content of general secondary education associated with qualitatively new access of students to the world's information resources, the use of multimedia tools as a tool in virtually all school academic disciplines.

It should also be noted that the expediency of practical application of such projects proves the essential didactic potential of modern telecommunication systems and corresponding multimedia resources used in teaching schoolchildren.

A student can join an educational project on his/her own if he/she is already trained to work with telecommunication systems and has the skills to use appropriate technical multimedia tools. When implementing the project method, all project activities are directed at the learner, and it is not so important whether the learner is involved in them at school or at home. Independence in the choice of learning trajectory allows the student to reach a new, higher level of work with the Internet and to consider the network as a tool of cognition and self-development, which, in turn, contributes to the manifestation of social activity of the student.

The distributed telecommunication multimedia resources used in schoolchildren's education can include various tools created for the general secondary education system and delivered to the learner through the use of a variety of telecommunication means.

In particular, such technologies may include distance technologies that use television networks and satellite channels of multimedia information transmission. Such educational technologies are based on the modular principle, which implies the division of the content of a school discipline into closed blocks, for which control activities are provided.

Monitoring of the quality of knowledge assimilation by pupils is realized with the help of the electronic testing system.

Modern telecommunication technologies and distributed multimedia educational resources placed on them are characterized by a wide use of computer-based training programs and electronic textbooks available to schoolchildren via global (Internet) and local (Intranet) computer networks. The element of learning in such technology is, first of all, the face-to-face forms of lessons and certification of schoolchildren. Therefore, it is more correct to speak about complex technologies with significant use of educational electronic publications and other distributed multimedia resources of telecommunication networks.

In this approach, all multimedia learning materials are placed on servers and are available for self-study. The learner has the opportunity to contact the teacher, take intermediate and final tests.

Multimedia resources and specialized methods of teaching students using such resources can bring the school:

- using multimedia information available on educational and scientific Web-sites to complete assignments, prepare teaching materials, essays, project works;

- organization of the school's representation on the Internet;

- creation of a multimedia resource on one of the school disciplines posted on the Internet;

- hosting personal Web sites of teachers and students.

Teaching methods should take into account that the entire WWW space consists of documents called Web pages. A Web page is a document that contains:

- formatted text;

- multimedia objects (graphics, sound, video clips);

- links to other Web pages or other Internet resources;

- active components capable of performing work on the client's computer according to a program embedded in them.

Within a single page is difficult to present all the necessary information, so, as a rule, the information is presented as a set of several dozen or hundreds of Web-pages, linked together by a common theme, a common style of design and mutual hypertext links. Such a set is called a Web-site or Web-node.

Web-site (Web-node, Web-site) - a group of Web-pages linked together by a common theme, common design style and mutual hypermedia links.

Every Web site has its own start page, which is called the initial or home page.

A normal Web node sends the requested multimedia resource only when requested by the client. There are Web nodes on the WWW that can send updated information on their own if the client registers and subscribes.

Numerous Web sites and Web pages are stored on a multitude of so-called WWW servers, i.e. computers on which special software is installed.

Users who have access to the network, receive and view information from Web-pages with the help of programs-clients for the World Wide Web, which are specifically called Web-browsers (browsers, browsers).

To receive a page, the browser sends a request via the computer network to the Web server where the required multimedia resource is stored. In response to the request, the server sends the viewer the required Web-page or a message of refusal, if it is for one reason or another unavailable. Interaction client-server occurs according to certain rules, or, in other words, the application protocol. The protocol adopted in the WWW is called HyperText Transfer Protocol, abbreviated as HTTP.

Web-document can contain formatted text, graphics and hypertext links to various Internet resources. To realize all these possibilities and to ensure the independence of multimedia resources of the World Wide Web from the system software of the personal computer on which they will be viewed, a special language was developed. It is called HyperText Markup Language (HTML) or Hypertext Markup Language.

An HTML document is a text-formatted file containing a set of commands (tags) that specify what information and in what form a Web page contains. Most often, an HTML file contains the text that is placed on a Web page.

Some tags describe the way the text is formatted, others indicate the embedded multimedia objects and other components of the Web document. All multimedia objects and other components of a Web page are stored in separate external files. There are special tags for creating hypertext links.

Each file on the Internet also has its own unique address. It is called a URL. URL (Universal Resource Locator). The URL contains the name of the protocol to access the file, the address of the computer with an indication of which server program to run on it, and the full path to the file.

Chapter 5.

Development of multimedia resources

§ 5.1 Requirements for educators developing and using multimedia resources

The use of modern multimedia technologies and specialized teaching tools based on diverse information cannot have a proper effect in the system of general secondary education without the formation of appropriate readiness of teachers. A modern teacher should possess all the knowledge, skills and abilities necessary for effective realization of his/her professional activity with the use of quality multimedia resources.

Effective teaching of schoolchildren using multimedia resources will be realized if a modern teacher possesses:

- general pedagogical skills;

- skills in multimedia tools and multimedia technologies;

- skills of application of information and telecommunication technologies and multimedia technologies in the system of general secondary education.

Teachers working in the system of general secondary education should know where and how to find educational multimedia resources in telecommunication networks, be able to use such networks in various aspects of teaching and learning, know how to present the content of educational subjects through multimedia technologies, and how to apply multimedia tools in teaching schoolchildren.

Effective mastering of the educational potential of multimedia tools presupposes appropriate training of the teacher, who should be based on the following provisions:

- training to work with educational multimedia resources is part of the content of teacher education;

- multimedia learning tools are only a tool for solving problems, the use of such tools and technologies should not become an end in itself;

- The use of multimedia tools expands the problem-solving capabilities of human thinking;

- Multimedia training is a mindset-building method.

As modern multimedia technologies are introduced into general secondary education, the culture of the school and the role of the teacher in the learning process are changing. Due to the emphasis on independent acquisition of knowledge, the advisory and corrective orientation of the teacher's teaching activity is intensified. In the conditions of excessive scientific and educational information provided to students by modern multimedia technologies, the requirements to the teacher's professional training in the field of basic and related academic disciplines are increasing. The requirements to personal, general cultural and communicative qualities of teachers also increase significantly.

Many school teachers still experience a significant psychological barrier before mastering computer technology and using multimedia resources in teaching, which is usually masked by doubts about the pedagogical possibilities of multimedia tools and multimedia technologies. Sometimes such underestimation is explained by superficial familiarity with the essence of the processes of informatization of education.

Even a superficial analysis shows that most often the introduction of multimedia into the teaching process is perceived as a simple transposition of the content known to the teacher and its presentation to students with the help of computer tools. It is obvious that this approach leaves unused the enormous opportunities for activation of visual and theoretical figurative thinking of schoolchildren.

One of the priority problems on the way of practical informatization of education and widespread use of educational multimedia teaching resources is the training of teaching staff. There are several priority tasks, the solution of which can have a positive effect in the process of formation of modern teachers' readiness to use multimedia resources in teaching. In particular, it is necessary to create a multilevel system of teachers' professional development.

From the point of view of education informatization, it is reasonable to divide all teachers into two main categories: teachers-users of ready multimedia resources and teachers-developers of multimedia tools for pedagogical purposes. In the course of forming the described readiness, the first category of teachers should be oriented to training up to the end-user level. A teacher should master elementary computer skills, get the first idea of the most common universal software packages, learn to work with text editors, spreadsheets, learn to work with ready-made multimedia resources known for his/her subject area, as well as systems of telecommunication interaction with colleagues and students, means of access to global sources of multimedia information.

The course of lectures on the psychological and pedagogical foundations of information educational technologies is recommended for teachers-users seeking to use multimedia tools in teaching. Practical implementation of such a course causes many different difficulties, since its content is located at the intersection of disciplines of the psychological and pedagogical cycle and disciplines related to software and hardware of computer and telecommunication technologies.

The training of the second category of teachers, which includes teachers who develop multimedia resources they need on their own, should be close to the level of training of qualified users or even programmers. This is essential for understanding and rationally designing the structure of multimedia resources. It is extremely important for teachers-developers to learn both the basics of designing and using multimedia learning tools and the basics of pedagogy and psychology required for this as part of professional development courses or on their own.

When developing multimedia resources, it should be taken into account that creative teams with the participation of system and application programmers, psychologists, designers, ergonomics specialists are a necessary, but not sufficient condition for quality development. The main concept, content and idea of an educational multimedia resource should be proposed and improved by the subject teacher. The teacher, in his turn, should proportion his ideas and conceptions with the specific capabilities of the used hardware, software, and the level of professional training of the development team.

Due to the fact that multimedia resources used in teaching are not only pedagogical, but also software tools, it is impossible to transfer the content of the course through them without careful structuring of the teaching material. Thus, for the rational design of multimedia learning tools for the whole course, teachers - developers need to have a structural and systemic holistic view of the material of the academic discipline, specialized tools and technologies for designing the content of multimedia learning tools according to the identified structures of the content of educational areas typical for the system of general secondary education.

School Teachers who are actively engaged in the development and use of multimedia tools should have a sufficient level of readiness to use educational informatization tools in the teaching process.

The requirements for a teacher using multimedia tools in teaching schoolchildren should consist of traditional requirements for any teacher and specific requirements related to the use of modern information technologies in the process of informatization of educational activities.

Traditional requirements include:

- organizational (planning of work, rallying of trainees, etc.);

- didactic (specific skills to select and prepare teaching material and equipment; accessible, clear, expressive, convincing and consistent presentation of teaching material; stimulating the development of cognitive interests and spiritual needs);

- perceptive (manifested in the ability to penetrate into the spiritual world of the educated, to objectively assess their emotional state, to identify the features of the psyche);

- communicative (ability to establish pedagogically appropriate relations with students, their parents, colleagues, heads of educational institution);

- Suggestive (emotional and volitional influence on students);

- research (ability to cognize and objectively evaluate pedagogical situations and processes);

- Scientific and cognitive (the ability to assimilate scientific knowledge in the chosen field);

- subject matter (professional knowledge of the subject of study).

In the case of using modern educational multimedia tools, such requirements are significantly transformed. At the same time, there are specific requirements necessary when working with modern means of informatization and multimedia resources. Such requirements include, for example, the teacher's knowledge of didactic properties and ability to use multimedia learning tools.

It is advisable to publish specialized editions designed to activate the interest of the pedagogical community in the problems of development and implementation of modern multimedia technologies. Such publications should be oriented to a wide range of specialists:

teachers of all areas and levels of training, administrators of general secondary education;

Teacher educators across disciplines;

specialists in various areas of computer science, such as human-computer interface, graphic applications, artificial intelligence, computer science, and telecommunications;

psychologists;

ergonomists;

sociologists;

linguists.

It is obvious that these publications can and should become a center of experience exchange, development and transfer of knowledge and skills, a link that unites the activities of all those who are engaged in the development and practical application of modern multimedia tools and resources.

One of the most effective active methods for future and present teachers to master the means of multimedia presentation of information are projects based on the construction of educational multimedia resources.

Among the many purposes of building and using multimedia resources in teacher education for general secondary education, two main groups can be distinguished:

formation of teachers' technological skills of working with modern telecommunication environments and multimedia resources;

formation of skills in the application of multimedia technologies in teaching schoolchildren.

To explain the selection of such groups, we note that, firstly, the teacher should acquire the necessary user technological skills of working with multimedia resources and Internet sites: the use of the main popular software tools (such as Front Page, Internet Explorer, Netscape Navigator, Outlook Express, etc.), search engines and catalogs of multimedia resources. Secondly, no less important and essential are the intellectual skills of working with information of various kinds: the ability to purposefully find the necessary multimedia information, to see the information in its entirety and not in fragments, to evaluate various psychological techniques of the impact of specific information on the student, to distinguish the correct argumentation, to critically reflect on the information, to save and use it in professional activities; to process and present the content of multimedia resources of the Internet; to conduct training at a high level of professionalism; to work with multimedia resources of the Internet; to work with multimedia resources of the Internet; to work with multimedia resources of the Internet; to work with multimedia resources of the Internet; to work with multimedia resources of the Internet; to work with multimedia resources of the Internet; to work with multimedia resources of the Internet.

During the training, educators should internalize the basic rules that should be considered when developing multimedia learning tools. These include:

▪ inclusion in educational multimedia tools of substantive and methodological hints, comments and explanations of various simulated situations;

▪ ensuring in the course of pedagogical use of multimedia information the stage of training with varying goals of each stage, starting from the formation of general ideas about multimedia technologies and telecommunications and ending with the formation of student's skills to independently present this or that multimedia information, the formation of general information culture;

▪ Targeting multimedia tools and resources to teach technological and intellectual skills in a personalized way,

▪ orientation on the formation of the ability to resist the negative impact of information technologies;

▪ use of multimedia tools that increase visibility and meet ergonomic requirements;

▪ clear definition of the teacher's position in the course of individualized practical use of multimedia resources: the choice of training tasks and techniques most suitable for different groups of students, taking into account the   individual characteristics of students and psychological features of information perception by them, the characteristics of the group and the nature of mutual assistance;

▪ The distance between the teacher and the learner and the conduct of problem discussions with the teacher in the role of a facilitator; maximum preservation of the interactive mode, solving educational tasks at an individual rhythm.

§ 5.2 Formation of educational content and system of concepts. Thesaurus

The selection of educational content and, as a consequence, the selection of the content of educational multimedia resources is currently a complex and urgent problem that constantly attracts the attention of scientists, methodologists and teachers. There is a large number of different approaches to teaching, in the process of development and implementation of which a specific language of educational disciplines is developed, the basic concepts of educational areas are identified, the content and structure of teaching are determined. The solution of the problem of content selection is complicated by the fact that nowadays in teaching almost all disciplines, in addition to textbooks and teaching aids, it is necessary to develop informatization tools aimed at the integrated use of computer technology in the learning process.

The initial issue that needs to be resolved is the distinction between the interpretations of the concepts of subject area and educational field, which should be the starting point for the further presentation.

Throughout the history of pedagogy the correlation between science and educational subject is studied, the formation of criteria for the selection of educational material on the basis of methodological analysis of the state and prospects of development of subject scientific branches. The educational subject is not the result of projecting the corresponding branch of science on learning, but the outcome of didactic processing of a certain system of knowledge, skills and abilities necessary for mastering intellectual, material-practical, social or spiritual activities.

Subject area is a set of concepts, knowledge and ideas of a scientific branch or branch of human activity. At the same time, the educational domain is understood as a subset of the subject area, taken as a basis for the content of educational activities and adapted to the psychological and age specificity of the contingent of students.

The approach to the formation of the content of a fixed educational area, significant for the construction of the content of multimedia resources is reduced to the following main stages:

1. Define the subject activity of the projected educational and cognitive activity: outline the range of objects involved in the cognitive activity and set a list of concepts, problems and methods from the perspective of which the selected range of objects will be studied;

2. Articulate the patterns to be learned in the academic discipline;

3. Evaluate the correlation between the components of the knowledge system related to the description, explanation of the studied phenomena, justification of the formulated regularities, with the performance of cognitive actions, prescriptions;

4. To formulate general provisions on the knowledge of which the formed educational discipline will be based;

5. Form a list of tasks, the fulfillment of which will serve as a criterion for mastering the content of the academic discipline;

6. Formulate a list of tasks that are significant in terms of the development of a particular professional teaching activity.

It is necessary to adhere to the following indicative step-by-step technology of forming the content of the subject:

1. Focusing on modern scientific works (monographs, articles, etc.) on the subject of study, it is necessary to build a logical structure of the content of this section of science;

2. Articulate the principles of content selection;

3. Based on these principles, select the necessary number of learning elements from

the formed content structure, build a logical structure of the subject (educational area) and make sure that the obtained learning elements are not excessive and sufficient to achieve the learning objectives.

In addition to the above-mentioned steps for the formation of the content of the educational area it is necessary to plan the study of possible levels of assimilation of the content material, justification of the absence of overload in the activities of students, to develop the required training material, presenting it with the help of multimedia technologies.

An essential element of multimedia resources content formation is the structuring of the educational domain. One of the possible methods in this case is to use the educational domain as a content base for structuring a set of concepts, the content of which should form the basis of the multimedia tool being created.

The development of a system of educational concepts is a key point in the process of selecting and forming the content of an educational discipline, as well as in the use of the selected content in the development of multimedia tools. It is noteworthy that the problems of correct selection of concepts are faced by specialists working in almost all scientific fields related to the modern educational process.

A concept is a logically formalized general thought or idea about a class of objects or phenomena. At the same time, a term is understood as a word or phrase expressing a special concept, which is correlated with other concepts in a given subject area and has a unique scientific definition.

The following factors should be considered in the term selection process:

■ it is necessary to correlate the term with its lexical equivalent correctly and as unambiguously as possible;

■ term cannot be free from the general context in which it is used;

■ for correct understanding of a term it is necessary to know its morphological structure, semantic features that distinguish it from commonly used words, the main types of terms, their structural features and specifics of use.

The preliminary definition of concept systems of the educational domain or its subset selected for the multimedia resource should be the first step in defining the learning content. The development of such a system, in its turn, consists of two integral components: the definition of the concepts themselves, which are the "framework" of the whole educational material, and the development of their structure - the identification of links between individual concepts.

It should be taken into account that the formation of concepts (or their assimilation) presupposes the subject's ability to organize the activity of identifying the properties inherent in some real objects or ideas. The ability to form concepts consists in the ability to find out the properties inherent in some class of objects or ideas. Orientation to the correct formation of concepts in the learner is one of the main components of the formation of the content of any educational area.

An important role in cognition is played by general concepts (categories), which are considered as initial concepts undefined through other concepts. In logic and systems theory, categories are such concepts as object, property, relation, judgment, inference, truth, system, environment, subject area, etc.

The selection of each concept should be based on important indicators such as:

- cognitive relevance and didactic value;

- correspondence to the content of science and its place in its theoretical system;

- Accessibility to learners;

- adequacy of materialized forms of expression of a concept to its content and interpretation;

- interrelation with other important concepts of the educational field;

- Ability to function optimally in training.

Let us consider some steps to construct a system of concepts, the use of which would be possible when creating multimedia resources. To build such a system, it is necessary to identify a natural-logical model of the studied subject area. This task cannot be solved by means of a specific academic discipline. It is solved by an expert on the basis of knowledge of the theory of the given subject area as a science: a system of concepts for a fixed educational area can be selected only on the basis of a scientific system of concepts, being a part of it.

The natural-logical model carries the most complete information about the image of a given evolving concept. However, some of this information can be given in implicit form. In contrast, the conceptual model allows to fully reveal both the content of the concept being defined and the way of including the defining concepts in it. It should be noted that already at this stage the question of structurization of concepts and identification of connections between them, at least on the principle of "parent" - "descendant", arises.

The construction of a correct system of concepts helps to simplify both the content of the educational area and the technology of its definition. However, an "overloaded" system of concepts with a high degree of nesting of terms can also play a negative role, greatly complicating and "confusing" the content. In principle, it is possible to build the structure of the educational field, bringing the division to undefinable axioms. At the same time, such division makes the structure too cumbersome. It is obvious that the number of levels or the complexity of the conceptual structure should be determined in each specific case, based on the learning objectives and, possibly, on the specifics and purposes of application of the educational multimedia tools being developed.

Concepts and various kinds of relations between them are called thesaurus. More precisely, a thesaurus is understood as a set of meaning-expressing elements (words, word combinations, etc.) of some language with specified semantic relations.

Simplistically, a thesaurus can be understood as a specific way of specifying a set of concepts and relations on it. For example, the traditional general language thesaurus was described as early as in Roget's dictionary. The key to the traditional thesaurus is an alphabetic dictionary, where for each word the rubrics containing it (and thus the words that are in synonymy with the data) are indicated. The structure of dividing the headings into subheadings defines generic relations on the set of words. The concept of thesaurus (Greek She/aigsh - treasure, wealth, stock) came to pedagogy from lexicography, where it emerged in connection with the creation of monolingual dictionaries in which words are grouped by semantic nests.

The formation of thesauruses of educational areas necessary for creating the content of multimedia resources can be carried out according to the following stages.

1. Identification of the main concepts of the educational field on the basis of literature analysis, their definition and compilation of a list of concepts, possibly in the form of a simple alphabetical list.

2. Identification of connections between concepts, determination of criteria for their classification, consideration of connections according to different criteria for composing relations.

3. Compiling a thesaurus - an interconnected description of the relationships between concepts.

4. Building a model of the system of concepts in the form of a hierarchical structure.

5. Identifying the need to augment definitions due to the design of relationships between concepts.

6. Checking the constructed conceptual structure for semantic closure, consistency and achievability.

7. Adjustment and clarification of the system of concepts of the educational field, development of conceptual provisions necessary in determining the content and development of teaching tools.

Formed thesauri should become a kind of raw material for the subsequent construction of educational domain structures and their processing in order to build educational multimedia resources.

When building a thesaurus of an educational area and using it in the creation of multimedia resources, the choice of a linking relation is determined by the goals, form and context of its subsequent application in the educational process in the system of general secondary education.

§ 5.3 Developing educational hypermedia resources

The use of hypertext technologies in the construction of educational multimedia tools can be closely related to the described approaches to thesaurus construction. Hierarchies of concepts with a glossary (alphabetical list), comments and additional hypermedia information are thesauri of educational fields. Such a thesaurus is almost identical to the thesaurus of a hypermedia tool: in both cases we deal with a set of concepts, links between them and some additional information.

In this connection, the process of obtaining an educational hypermedia resource (and even a traditional "paper" textbook) can be reduced to a sufficiently formalized and computer-processable process of traversing the hierarchical structure with generation for each node of the tree (thesaurus concept) of a corresponding information article containing hyperlinks according to the edges of the hierarchy (links between thesaurus concepts) and information presented in additional multimedia files. In this case, the name of the hierarchy node should coincide with the title of the thesaurus hypermedia article, which, in turn, should be identical to the title of the corresponding information article.

When constructing and editing the hierarchy and alphabetical list, it is possible to use unrestricted names to define the concepts of the educational domain. They can be words, phrases, and even complete, complete sentences. In this case, these "verbose" names of nodes will be used for titles of thesaurus and information articles of hypermedia.

The thesaurus of an educational field, containing a multitude of concepts and the connections between them, represents the semantic basis that should be communicated to the student as a result of the learning process. In this regard, the content of any learning tools, including multimedia resources, should be built in strict accordance with such information hierarchies. However, practice shows that this is not enough for a normal learning process. There is a need for additional educational multimedia materials, which could be used to inform the learner about the features of the information base contained in the thesaurus of the educational field. The content, volume and type of such multimedia material should vary depending not only on the specifics of the educational field, but also on the individual characteristics of a particular contingent of students.

It is necessary to supplement the elements of the hierarchical structure with various information objects built according to the principles of hypermedia and multimedia. More precisely, each vertex of the hierarchical structure has some set of attributes, which include vertex parameters, comments and a set of additional files attached to the vertex. Additional files can be files of almost all known information formats and contain multimedia information - simple or formatted text, drawings, schemes, tables, diagrams, photos, audio or video recordings, test questions or answers, etc. The presence or absence of attached files has no influence on the presence or absence of attached files. The presence or absence of attached files does not affect the structure of concepts in any way, but together with it it represents a system of necessary information components for the development of educational multimedia resources. The content of the attached files is used to compose the content of the hypermedia page of the multimedia resource corresponding to the given concept of the hierarchy.

In addition to the standard requirements imposed on any hypermedia resource, educational multimedia tools created with the help of thesauri should also obey specialized requirements, compliance with which occurs during the processing of hierarchies. In particular, in a hypermedia tool, along with information pages and possibly an index, there should be a page with the structure of the content of the tool, the so-called map, which is a hierarchy of titles of all pages of an educational multimedia resource or a structured table of contents. Each element of this hierarchy should be a hyperlink to the corresponding page of the multimedia resource being developed.

When constructing educational hypermedia tools, the features of construction and all other pages of such tools are regulated, which forms a system of hypertext navigation. The title of each hypermedia page contains the name of the corresponding top of the hierarchical structure, which is an element of the thesaurus of the educational domain. All hyperlinks intended for navigation through the multimedia tool should be grouped on the screen into three main groups.

The first group (the "parent" group) contains a single hyperlink to the page corresponding to the parent vertex with respect to the given vertex-page. In other words, this group contains a hyperlink to a page about the encompassing concept. The fact that this group always contains only one hyperlink is due to the previously described peculiarities of data organization in the form of a hierarchical tree, when each vertex can have no more than one parent. It follows that the group of "parents" can never be empty (this would contradict the property of tree connectivity), except, perhaps, for the very first, the main title page of an educational hypermedia tool, although it, as a rule, contains links to other, more comprehensive multimedia resources.

The second group (the "sons" group) contains hyperlinks to pages whose content clarifies or supplements the content of the current page. In the hierarchical structure of concepts, such hyperlinks correspond to descendant nodes for which the given node is the parent. Such selection of hyperlinks gives rise to a rather convenient methodology of viewing hypertext pages, when the learner does not proceed to the consideration of the material of a lower level. If the content of the current hypertext information article did not interest him or turned out to be known to him, and, conversely, in case the material of the hypertext article turned out to be useful or interesting for the user, he can use explicitly prescribed and grouped titles of hypertext articles containing more detailed material on this information area. There may be situations when the "sons" group does not contain any hyperlinks. The emptiness of this group indicates that the learner has reached the leaf of the corresponding hypertext hierarchy. In other words, for the content of a hypertext article that has an empty set of hyperlinks in the "sons" group, there is no clarifying or supplementary material in this educational hypermedia tool.

Finally, the third group (the group of "brothers") of hyperlinks points to pages whose information has the same semantic level as the current page, which corresponds to the vertices - brothers in the hierarchy. In other words, such a group contains a list of titles of hypertext articles that contain, in relation to the currently viewed page, similar in meaning material or material on a related "subject". Thus, to familiarize himself with all the concepts - representatives of this level of the hierarchy, the learner only needs to sequentially view all the "pages-brothers", which are indicated by hyperlinks from the third group. The group of "brothers" can not be empty, because it always contains at least one specially marked hyperlink to the very page being viewed at the moment. This provides the learner with additional information about the position of the page he is viewing in the semantic hierarchy "parent" - "brothers" - "sons".

Such distribution of hyperlinks on the pages of the educational hypermedia medium allows us to speak about the existence of the principle of dynamic change of hyperlinks during the transition from one hypertext page to another. When changing the semantic level (in relation to the semantic order set by the original hierarchy of concepts) associated with user transitions between hypertext pages, the system of hyperlinks visualized on the screen changes: it still has the three groups mentioned above, but the hyperlinks themselves either move between groups, or disappear from the screen as irrelevant to this semantic level. For example, when you go to any of the hyperlinks in the group "sons", the hyperlink from the group "parent" is replaced by a hyperlink to the hypertext page just viewed, hyperlinks in the group "brothers" are replaced by a set of hyperlinks that before the transition highlighted in the group "sons". In turn, the group of "sons" is completely updated in accordance with the structure of the corresponding subtree of the hierarchy associated with the top, which is the image of the thesaurus concept, the meaning of which is revealed in the current information article of the educational hypermedia tool.

The use of such a principle in the automatic generation of multimedia resources allows students to easily navigate through the information offered to them: when studying a particular multimedia material, they can, if necessary, elaborate on it, look through the description of similar concepts, or go to the content material that is comprehensive in meaning. It is obvious that such a methodology of working with multimedia information is aimed at increasing individualization of the learning process in the system of general secondary education.

In addition, teachers and students have at their disposal an algorithm for viewing all pages of an educational hypermedia tool, when all pages - sons - are viewed for one page, and then a transition to the page-brother is made. If viewing of pages-brothers and their corresponding subtrees ends, the transition to the parent page is made and the cycle of viewing is repeated for the parent's brother. Studying a concept by reading the corresponding information article, the learner sees the list of related concepts, the encompassing concept and concepts subordinate in meaning to the studied concept. When navigating through the multimedia resource in this way, the learner not only gets acquainted with all the hypermedia information, but also gets a complete picture of inter-conceptual semantic relations for the given educational area.

It is obvious that the creation of educational hypermedia tools with such properties is in no way tied to the peculiarities of educational areas, content and other components of existing methodological teaching systems existing in general secondary education. Regardless of the types of school subjects or types of educational activities typical for a modern school, their informatization becomes possible on the basis of hypermedia tools that implement the described principle of dynamic change of hyperlinks. In this case, teachers and students have at their disposal a single invariant principle of navigation through informatization tools, a single principle of selection and visualization of multimedia information, single principles of operation with multimedia tools, as well as a single principle of using the corresponding informatization tools in the educational process.

When using the described technology, the construction and operational change of an educational multimedia resource takes place in the mode of working with a hierarchical model of the structure of its content and its subsequent processing. Automation of the processes of creating and adjusting hypermedia learning tools allows replacing the usual work of writing texts in special languages with the creation of hierarchical structures and their corresponding information hypermedia supplements. Any subsequent change in the content of a multimedia resource is reduced to an explicit correction of its structure or joining the existing hierarchy of necessary information hypermedia elements and subsequent "reassembly" of the multimedia resource.

§ 5.4 Designing and developing the interface of educational multimedia resources

The development of design and interface of educational multimedia resources is as important as the formation of the content of such tools.

Observations conducted by teachers and psychologists show that the effectiveness of computer-based training programs is largely determined by the nature of the program interface. The design of multimedia resources has the most direct impact on students' motivation, speed of material perception, fatigue and a number of other important indicators. Therefore, the interface design of the learning environment should not be developed on an intuitive level. A scientifically grounded, balanced and thoughtful systematic approach is required.

Recommendations on the formation of the interface of educational multimedia tools can be divided into several main groups:

- recommendations on the application of a systematic approach to the design of multimedia resources;

- recommendations on the structure and content of the core learning elements;

- recommendations for organizing search, navigation and hyperlinking systems;

- recommendations for taking into account physiological features of perception of colors and shapes by schoolchildren;

- recommendations on the use of design elements.

The system approach to the interface formation is the basis of system design - a special type of creative design, which includes in the created multimedia resource all the factors that in any degree affect the process of its development and creation, the conditions of its subsequent functioning in the system of general secondary education. The logical conditionality of each subsequent step in the chain allows us to guarantee with the highest probability an adequate solution to the eternal problem of design - the ratio between the utilitarian (efficiency, economy, comfort) and the beautiful (aesthetic expressiveness, imagery, ability to evoke positive emotions and associations).

The system approach to the formation of the interface makes it possible to attract, in addition to traditional book studies, the achievements of such scientific areas as the theory of information, document, informatics, text linguistics, etc. This allows us to use a whole set of categories - functional, structural, historical, communicative, component, value, sociological, statistical, etc.

The principle of systematicity ensures various types of information structuring without loss of quality by using the achievements of modern science of signs and sign systems - semiotics. According to the semiotic approach, each sign system, such as a multimedia resource, should be studied taking into account the allocation of syntactic, semantic and pragmatic subsystems.

Experimental studies have established that:

- The difficulty of comprehension increases as the basic composition of words with more than 3 syllables increases;

- short-term memory capacity is 7 ± 2 units (unrelated digits, unrelated syllables or words);

- the productivity of meaningful memorization is 20 times higher than mechanical memorization;

- the bandwidth of the human visual analyzer is about 100 times greater than that of the auditory analyzer;

- The contextual environment of the underlying information directly affects the speed and accuracy of its recognition and perception;

- The configuration of spatial stimuli is important for the representation in visual short-term memory of information about the spatial location, color, and shape of stimuli.

When developing a multimedia resource, it is necessary to find an optimal combination of syntactic, semantic and pragmatic subsystems in the unified system of a multimedia medium, both in general and at all possible levels of its typological model.

In the design project the developer of an educational multimedia tool lays down the future unity of the target orientation, content and formal qualities of the object. The less logical, less functionally sound was the developed project, the more differences between the concept and the obtained product, the less effective the system is. The first phase of system design plays an important role. At this stage, the necessary information is collected and analyzed, which determines the semantic center of the subsequent activity.

The design concept justifies the goals of the project and the ways to achieve them. It is like the foundation of the future building, defining its functional and aesthetic possibilities. The student is always the driving force behind the design concept of a multimedia resource.

The design program acts as the initial phase of design. It contains the main groups of operations for the realization of the design concept and represents the actual project or model of this type of activity.

The design scenario concretizes the design program in the spatio-temporal environment and represents the scheme of the future multimedia resource, which allows to "play" all possible plots of its life activity.

The development of multimedia resources for general secondary education should also take into account specific recommendations concerning the interface design. For example, in order to move freely within the multimedia resource, learners need to have a response time of less than a second when moving from one page to another.

When developing a multimedia resource, students should not have to wait more than 10 seconds for a page to load, as this is the limit of a person's ability to focus on something while waiting.

Basic information regarding response times is given in a paper by Robert B. Miller at the Fall Joint Computer Conference back in 1968:

One tenth of a second (0.1) is the limit so that the response of the system received by the learner in this time would be perceived as instantaneous, i.e., requiring no feedback to display the results on the screen. This value should be the response time limit in multimedia resources that allow learners to move, resize, and otherwise manipulate elements on the screen in real time.

One second (1.0) is the maximum length of time during which the learner's train of thought is not interrupted, even if the learner notices a delay. Typically, feedback is not required if the delays are greater than 0.1 and less than 1 second, but the learner no longer feels that he or she is working directly on the data. If a new page appears within 1 second, it means that the learner is not experiencing excessive delays.

Ten seconds (10.0) is the limit during which the learner is focused on the dialog. If the delay is longer, the learner starts doing other things while waiting for the multimedia resource to end. The learner continues to follow links if new pages appear within 20 seconds.

The response time should be minimized. But it should be remembered that a computer can respond at a speed that is simply not comparable to the speed of the learner. For example, a scrolling list in a multimedia resource may move so fast that the learner may not be able to stop it in time for the desired item to remain on the screen.

In addition to speed, a small variation in response time is also important. Response times vary greatly when using multimedia resources, so students feel uncomfortable with slowness. The satisfaction of the learners depends not only on the response time but also on the expectations of the learners themselves. If the same action is sometimes fast and sometimes slow, learners do not know what to expect and therefore cannot act in a way that optimizes their performance. If trainees expect an action to be fast, they are confused by the fact that it is slow; on the other hand, if they expect an action to be slow, they are more relaxed about the same delay. This is why it makes sense to minimize all differences in response time. If it always takes the same amount of time to perform the same action, then the learner will know how long to wait.

You should help trainees to predict the loading time of large pages and files when using a multimedia resource. To do this, simply specify the size of the file or page to be downloaded next to the link. As a rule, the size should be specified for files that take longer than 10 seconds to load. It is worth warning about the size of any file larger than 50 Kbytes.

§ 5.5 Methods of using the developed multimedia resources

Let us consider possible methods of effective application of multimedia resources obtained as a result of building and processing thesauri of educational areas. In general, the following methods of using multimedia resources can be extended to almost all means of informatization of general secondary education.

It is obvious that the use of such tools and corresponding methodological developments is possible in cases where there is interaction of participants of the educational process with different types of information.

An essentially new teaching method, the realization of which is possible only on the basis of multimedia tools created as a result of processing thesauruses of educational areas, is the work of students with the content of the same educational area, the concepts and terms of which are structured according to different criteria. To realize this teaching methodology, several hierarchical structures of concepts are built for a fixed educational area, the number of which varies depending on the learning objectives.

Such hierarchical structures can be identified in several ways. For example, it is possible to use fundamentally different criteria for determining the links between concepts when constructing the initial graph-thesaurus of the educational domain. Further operation with such graphs is traditional. As another way of defining several hierarchies, it can be proposed to select several possible hierarchy trees for one pre-built thesaurus graph, which are essential from the point of view of understanding different approaches to describing the structure of the educational domain.

In any case, teachers have the opportunity to build several different hierarchies for the same system of educational concepts. It is not recommended to change the content of files with additional hypermedia information, built in advance for the nodes of one of such hierarchies, when attaching them to the nodes of the hierarchy built according to other criteria.

The creation of multimedia tools for several hierarchical structures will lead to the creation of "semi-finished products", the subsequent finalization of which will lead to the appearance of identical educational multimedia resources, the content and system of concepts of which corresponds to the same educational field, but the hierarchical structures that determine the layout and navigation characteristics of both multimedia tools will be different.

In the future, the built multimedia teaching tools of the same school discipline are presented to the students for their work. The methods of operation with such tools can be different depending on specific methodological systems, terms and conditions of training. In any case, the study of the same type of content information with the help of multimedia resources will lead to the achievement of two essential goals of the implementation of such methodological scenarios - familiarization of students with the content of the educational field and possible approaches and criteria for structuring its conceptual system. The essential result of this methodology application will be the formation of students' understanding of the influence of different approaches and criterion selection on information structurization.

For a more complete and effective practical use of multimedia tools created as a result of thesaurus processing, teachers can use certain methodological recommendations for the preparation of educational multimedia material.

In this case, the teacher prepares a so-called instructional block, the content of which includes a curriculum and a guide to the study of the discipline, focused on the qualitative composition and basic functionality of available educational multimedia resources. Next, an "electronic" lecture is compiled, the content of which is presented using similar means. The volume of information included in the lecture is equal to the volume of content of the traditional part of the school lesson, in which the teacher explains new material, and the number of blocks is equal to the number specified in the thematic plan. The structure of the content of each lecture includes:

An introduction to the lecture, explicitly listing what the student will know and be able to do after the lecture;

■ learning information itself, which is uniformly presented with the help of multimedia resources;

■ in case of psychological and pedagogical expediency, the lecture may include hyperlinks, audio, video fragments (production and scenarios of their use are agreed upon separately), additional means of informatization on the subject of the discipline, embedded in the content blocks within the lecture;

■ conclusions.

The next possible methodological step towards the introduction of multimedia resources into the teaching process could be the development of a specialized "electronic" seminar. As in the case of a lecture, the content information volume characteristic of such a seminar should be approximately equal to the similar content volume of the traditional practical part of the lesson. The number of thematic blocks of the seminar should be equal to the number provided by the thematic plan. Each block of the e-seminar has its own structure, the main components of which should be the topic of the seminar, the educational issues considered and the list of literature used.

The teacher's work with multimedia resources should begin with analyzing the results of students' work on studying the corresponding thematic blocks. At the next stage, the teacher should determine the level of each student's mastery of the content of educational material from the sections and topics of the block consisting of the previously described "electronic" lectures and seminars. In this case, an individual approach is possible, according to which the teacher develops private tasks for each student to prepare for work with educational multimedia tools that provide pedagogical control and measurement.

Further, depending on the level of students' readiness to work with specific multimedia tools, the teacher chooses the method of conducting the practical part of the lesson: seminar, game, training, etc. At the same time, the teacher should be obliged to analyze the possibilities of using multimedia resources of research and extracurricular nature available due to the possibility of using a telecommunication network. It is not excluded cases when the use of such resources in the educational process can become an additional factor in increasing its effectiveness.

While working with all, without exception, multimedia tools, the teacher should constantly compare the goals and results of students' learning of the content material planned by the curriculum in accordance with the syllabus.

The trainees' work with the developed multimedia tools should start with the accompanying documentation - the manual. In many cases, a single study of the manual for one multimedia tool may be sufficient to acquire knowledge about the specifics of operation of other similar tools. At this stage, the trainee must familiarize himself with the curriculum and understand the requirements for studying the content of the academic discipline, identify the list of multimedia tools that are expedient to use, note and express unresolved questions to the teacher, and get answers to them.

A rational, didactically grounded methodology of the learner's work with specific educational multimedia resources can be reduced to the following main stages:

- learning and understanding the information presented in the content of multimedia tools;

- passing tests (with the use of multimedia tools) in all thematic areas planned by the teacher;

- preparation for work with interactive publications and multimedia resources that require active creative activity of the learner;

- fulfillment of individual assignments of the teacher;

- participation in a practical training session (e-seminar, game, training);

- participation in extracurricular activities related to the studied thematic area and computerized on the basis of educational multimedia resources.

In addition to the described advantages of multimedia tools used in training, we should not forget about one more obvious functional and methodological opportunity of information and telecommunication technologies brought to the process of training schoolchildren. The point is that with the use of traditional methodology and means of teaching (textbook, task book, visual aid) the learning rate depends mainly on the average features of the group of students. With the use of the described capabilities of multimedia resources, the rate of learning depends on the individual characteristics of the learner and increases due to the organization of communication between the user and the multimedia medium in real time. At the same time, not only quantitative, but also qualitative composition of multimedia resources included as learning tools in a particular methodological system can be subjected to individual variation and adaptation.

Such opportunities for individualization of learning appear when using multimedia resources, as well as when implementing specialized teaching methods due to the visualization of educational information, storage of large amounts of information with the possibility of its transfer, easy access of teachers and students to the required data, information retrieval activities, automation of processing the results of experimental activities, control over the results of learning information, specialized uniform interactive dialogue.

The main aspects and advantages of using multimedia tools derived from the processing of thesauri of educational areas, significant from the methodological point of view, can be emphasized:

1. Any type of learning activity is accompanied by a parallel familiarization with the structure of the content of the educational area;

2. The content material provided to the learner is guaranteed to be free of semantic looping;

3. The learning methodology (trajectory) is determined on the basis of a predetermined unified algorithm of sequential traversal of the content sections of the multimedia tool, corresponding to the algorithm of traversal of the vertices of the hierarchical structure;

4. A new possibility of comparative study of different structures of the same concepts, as well as of the same content material structured according to different criteria is acquired;

5. The uniformity of approaches to the selection and presentation of the content of subject and educational areas, control and evaluation of students' actions, construction of interface and technological tools reduces the amount of material required to master the rules of operation with various multimedia tools;

6. It is possible to use the same multimedia tools and multimedia technologies to realize passive activity of students to study new content material and active creativity to design information resources.

All the noted methodological innovations indicate that the use of multimedia tools and multimedia technologies, in general, brings new teaching methods in the system of general secondary education, which cannot but affect the improvement of the quality of training of students, graduate students and teachers.

Conclusion

The methodological manual consists of 5 sections, is oriented to prepare teachers for reasonable and effective use of multimedia tools and technologies in distance learning of teachers, students and graduate students.

In the "Law on Education of the Republic of Kazakhstan" 2007 it is noted that "Taking into account the accumulated experience in the field of electronic and distance learning, the basic guidelines of the long-term program of education development up to 2020 in terms of education informatization are defined. This program envisages that by 2020 Kazakhstan's education system will function as part of a unified world information and educational space. At the same time, the technologicalization of the educational process, its personalization with orientation on an individual learning path, openness and accessibility of education will be ensured". Informatization of education on the basis of world achievements in the field of IT-technologies will be a means of innovative advanced development of Kazakhstani education. Many universities of the Republic of Kazakhstan, when introducing information technologies in the management of the educational process, face the lack of suitable open source software, as well as the high cost of available on the market automation solutions for universities. One of the main advantages is universality in terms of organizing the learning process - Moodle implements a learning environment in which students can interact with learning materials, with teachers and with each other. This is the key to the versatility of Moodle, allowing to apply this system to organize a variety of different types of training in different types of organizations. For example, one of the leading universities in Kazakhstan that use e-learning technology in the educational process is the Kazakh National Technical University named after K.I. Satpayev. Distance learning is a promising model of learning based on the use of new multimedia technologies and the Internet to improve the quality of learning by facilitating access to resources and services, as well as sharing and collaborative work at a distance. All advanced educational systems in the world are already focused on distance learning. e-Learning is progressing at a great pace with the support of UNESCO and other organizations whose activities are aimed at promoting education and increasing access to it for people in the information society. In addition, e-learning is seen as the primary means of lifelong learning, which is an integral part of building and operating a knowledge-based society.

Literature

1. Development of the Institute of Distance Education, Peoples' Friendship University of Russia, 2006; http://www.ido.rudn.ru/nfpk/ikt/; *STRUCTURE OF CONTENT of educational electronic Internet publication for teachers; Authors: Sergey Grigoriev; Vadim Grinshkun, Vadim Valerievich*

2. **USE OF MULTIMEDIA TECHNOLOGIES IN GENERAL MEDIUM EDUCATION** 20.10.2006 10:57 | N.A.Savchenko http: //www.ido .rudn.nfpk/ru/nfpk/mult/autor.html;

3. Benno A. On the organization of group work and the choice of tasks for it. // Soviet pedagogy and school. / Tartu, - 1972. C. 93-104.

4. Bespalko V.P. Theory of textbook. Didactic aspect. // M.: Pedagogy, - 1988. 160 c.

5. Bespalko V.P. Constituents of pedagogical technology. // M.: Pedagogy, - 1989. 192 c.

6. Bondarenko A.K. Education of children in the game. // M.: Prosveshchenie, - 1983. 137 c.

7. Bruner J. Psychology of cognition. // M.: Progress, - 1977. 412 c.

8. Vekker L.M. Psikhika i Reality: Unified Theory of Mental Processes. // M.: Smysl; Per Se, - 2000. 685 c.

9. Verbitsky A.A. Active learning in higher school: contextual approach. // M., - 1991.

10. Volkova V.V. Design of advertising. // M.: University, - 1999.

11. Ginetsinsky V.I. Fundamentals of theoretical pedagogy. // SPb.: Izd-vo SPbSU, - 1992. 154 c.

12. Grigoriev S.G., Grinshkun V.V.. Informatization of education - new educational discipline. // In Proceedings of the XVI International Conference "Application of New Technologies in Education". Troitsk: MPE FNTO "Baytik", - 2005. C. 102-104.

13. Grigoriev S.G., Grinshkun V.V. On the development of the textbook "Informatization of Education". // Bulletin of Moscow State Pedagogical University. Series of informatics and informatization of education. / M.: MGPU, - 2005, №1 (4), P. 24-28.

14. Grigoriev S.G., Grinshkun V.V. Textbook - a step on the way to the system of teaching "Informatization of education". // In the collection of scientific papers "Problems of school textbook". / Scientific and methodological edition. M.: ISMO RAO, - 2005. C. 219222.

15. Dergacheva L.M. Activization of schoolchildren's learning activity when studying informatics on the basis of using didactic games. // Author's thesis of Cand. ped. sciences. / M., - 2006.

16. Jaja V.P. The method of thematic immersion when using multimedia technologies in teaching mathematics (on the example of trigonometry). // Dissertation of Candidate

of Ped. sciences. / M. - 2005. 180 c.

17.   Didactics of Secondary School: Some Problems of Modern Didactics. Textbook for students of FPC for principals of general education schools and as a textbook for a special course for students of pedagogical institutes. // Edited by M.N. Skatkin. / 2nd edition, revision and supplement. M.: Prosveshchenie, - 1982.

18.   Donskoy M. Internet and user interface. //World of Internet. - 1999. № 9.

19.   Informatics and Education. //M.: Education and Informatics, - 20O2, №№5,6,8,9, 2003, №2.

20.   Artificial Intelligence and Psychology. // Ed. by O.K. Tikhomirov. / M.: Nauka, - 1976. 343 c.

21.   Kudryashova T.G. Systemic use of multimedia teaching tools: problems and ways to solve them. // Bulletin of Moscow State Pedagogical University. Series "Informatics and informatization of education". / M.: MGPU, - 2004. № 1(2). C. 94-101.

22.   Levina O.G. Interaction of computer and human as a social phenomenon. // Pedagogical Bulletin. M., - 1998. №2.

2 3.Ozhegov S.I., Shvedova N.Y. Tolkovoi Dictionary of the Russian Language: 80 000 words and phraseological expressions. // Russian Academy of Sciences. V.V. Vinogradov Institute of Russian Language. Vinogradov. / 4th edition, supplemented. M.: Azbukovnik, - 1999, 944 p.

24.   Polat E.S. New pedagogical and information technologies in the education system. // M.: Publishing Center "Academy". - 2003. 272 c.

25.   Polat E.S., Buharkina M.Y., Moiseeva M.V., Petrova A.E. New pedagogical and information technologies in education: Textbook for students of pedagogical universities and the system of advanced training of pedagogical staff. // M.: Publishing Center "Academy". - 2002. 147 c.

26.   Polschikova O.N. Use of business games in teaching the school course of informatics. // Autoref. diss. kand. ped. nauk. / M., - 2005.

27.   Sergeeva T. New information technologies and the content of training. // Informatics and Education. M., - 1991. №1. C. 310.

28.   Skatkin M.N. Class-lesson system. // Russian Pedagogical Encyclopedia: In 2 vol. / Ed. by V.V.Davydov. - Moscow: Big Russian Encyclopedia, Vol. 1, - 1993. C. 444.

29.   Subbotin M.M. Use of the computer in the construction of meaningful reasoning. // Scientific and Technical Information. Ser. 2. M., - 1986. №11.

30.   Subbotin M.M. New information technology: creation and processing of hypertext. // Scientific and Technical Information. Ser. 2. M., - 1988. №5.

31.   Subbotin M.M. Theory and practice of non-linear writing (a view through the prism of J. Derrida's "grammatology"). // Questions of Philosophy. M., - 1993. №3. C. 36-45.

32.   Shvetsky M.V. Methodical system of fundamental training of future teachers of

informatics in pedagogical university in the conditions of two-stage education. // Autoref. dis. dr. of pedagogical sciences. / Spb.: Russian State Pedagogical University - 1994. 36 c.

33.   Shiyanov E.N., Kotova I.B. Development of personality in learning: Textbook for students of universities. // M.: Publishing Center "Academy", - 1999. 288 c.

34.   Goldstein I.P. The Genetic Graph: Representation for the Evolution of Procedural Knolledge. // Int. G. of Men-machine Studies, - 1979, No. 11, P. 51-77.

35.   Grigoriev S., Grinshkun V. Informational technologies in education as separate direction of preparing a pedagogical personnel. // "Information Technologies and Telecommunications in Education and Science IT&T ES'2005" Materials of the International Scientific Conference. / SIIT&T Informika - Moscow: VIZCOM, Ege Uneversity, Izmir, Turkey - 2005, P. 98101.

I want morebooks!

Buy your books fast and straightforward online - at one of world's fastest growing online book stores! Environmentally sound due to Print-on-Demand technologies.

Buy your books online at
www.morebooks.shop

Kaufen Sie Ihre Bücher schnell und unkompliziert online – auf einer der am schnellsten wachsenden Buchhandelsplattformen weltweit! Dank Print-On-Demand umwelt- und ressourcenschonend produzi ert.

Bücher schneller online kaufen
www.morebooks.shop

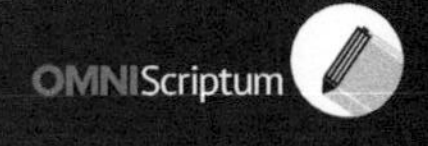

Printed by Books on Demand GmbH, Norderstedt / Germany